MONETARY AND EXCHANGE RATE POLICIES 1960-2001

The Experience of Somalia

By

Mohamed Dalmar Abdurahman

authorHOUSE™

1663 LIBERTY DRIVE, SUITE 200
BLOOMINGTON, INDIANA 47403
(800) 839-8640
WWW.AUTHORHOUSE.COM

First published by AuthorHouse 06/13/05

ISBN: 1-4208-1355-2 (sc)

Library of Congress Control Number: 2004099371

Printed in the United States of America
Bloomington, Indiana

This book is printed on acid-free paper.

TABLE OF CONTENTS

TABLES

FIGURES

BOX

PREFACE

This is the second edition of the book, *Monetary and Exchange Rate Policy 1960-2001, the Experience of Somalia.* The first edition was published in 2003 as a booklet. An earlier, shorter edition was also published in 1998. The present edition contains extensive revisions and updates to reflect recent developments in Somali financial markets.

Originally, the study was written as my master's thesis for a graduate program in administration conducted jointly between the Somali Institute of Development Administration and Management and the State University of New York at Albany in 1990.

This book is intended for students of the Somali economy as well as for policymakers. It is an attempt to document and explain the monetary history of Somalia in the last forty years—a history characterized by financial chaos and disorder. The aim is to provide some insight into this history in the hope that some lessons will be drawn from it.

I have tried to use as little jargon as possible and have provided a glossary of economic terms at the end of the book for the benefit of the reader.

I would like to thank my instructor, David McCaffrey, who supervised the original study. I also thank Ali Khalif Galayr, who encouraged me to publish the original study, and Abdisalam Isse-Salwe who provided me with some useful comments. I am also grateful to the administrators of Hiiraan-OnLine Web site for allowing me to publish the pictures of the ruined buildings of the Central Bank of Somalia and of the Commercial and Savings Bank of Somalia.

ABBREVIATIONS AND ACRONYMS

AFIS	Amministrazione Fiduciaria Italiana della Somalia (Italian Administration on the Trust Territory of Somalia)
CBS	Central Bank of Somalia
CCMS	Cassa per la Circolazione Monetaria della Somalia
CSBS	Commercial and Savings Bank of Somalia
FAO	Food and Agriculture Organization
IGAD	Intergovernmental Authority on Development
ILO	International Labour Organization
IMF	International Monetary Fund
IRIN	Integrated Regional Information Network
PPP	Purchasing Power Parity
SoSh.	Somali shilling
SlSh.	Somaliland shilling
TNG	Transitional National Government
UNCTAD	United Nations Conference on Trade and Development
UNDOS	United Nations Development Office for Somalia
UNDP	United Nations Development Programme
UNISOM	United Nations Operation in Somalia

INTRODUCTION

During the 1980s and the 1990s, the Somali shilling had suffered from large and continuous devaluations. These devaluations, in turn, added to inflationary pressure, eroded the purchasing power of money, and caused a chaotic financial situation that, according to some observers, was the decisive factor contributing to the downfall of General Mohamed Siad Barre's government.

To underscore the importance of exchange rates, Professor Robert Mundell, a renowned international currencies expert and 1999 Nobel Prize winner for economics, warned, "If there is a single issue that could lead to the breakup of Canada, it's the exchange rate." He argued that Quebec might realize that it could be better off by fixing an independent currency to the U.S. dollar instead of sharing an unstable Canadian dollar.[1] Lately, there has been a public debate over the future of the Canadian dollar, with some advocating for fixed exchange rates, others proposing the outright adoption of the U.S. dollar, and still others defending the status quo. In Argentina, many analysts blame the exchange rates for the social explosion that erupted in that country in December 2001, which caused the resignation of the president and the fleeing of the minister of finance for his life after two days of riots, arson, looting, and the death of at least twenty-seven people. Argentina's mistake was that it hung on for too long to an inflexible exchange rate system. Ecuador, Guatemala, and El Salvador have gone so far as to scrap their national currencies in favor of the U.S. dollar. In Europe, euro notes and coins were introduced in January 2002 to eliminate the exchange rates of the twelve national currencies.

---

[1] Interview with *The Ottawa Citizen*, July 25, 1998.

What is the exchange rate? And why it so important? The exchange rate is the price of a currency in terms of other currencies. It is perhaps the single most important price in the economy, as it affects the relative prices of domestic and foreign goods. In fact, the exchange rate is regarded as a barometer, which measures the relative strength of an economy over time. Well-performing and successful economies are judged by the strength and firmness of their currencies, while less successful and crisis-ridden economies are associated with soft and depreciating currencies. The fact that the Somali shilling had depreciated from SoSh. 6.23 per U.S. dollar in early 1970s to SoSh.6,000 at the end of 1990 is held as a proof of the gross economic mismanagement by the previous government. Likewise, the phenomenal fall in the value of the shilling to 22,500 shillings per U.S. dollar by December 2001 is yet an indication of how devastated is the economy of Somalia after eleven years of civil war and anarchy.

The exchange rate is also important because it profoundly affects the standard of living of the population. In a small, open economy like Somalia, where almost everything is imported, a depreciating currency raises the domestic prices of imported goods, most of which are foodstuffs, and thus reduces the purchasing power of money, and finally erodes the real income of the population. This hurts mostly the poor, who lack the means to protect themselves from the ravages of devaluation. Equally, the poor suffer the most when social services are slashed following structural adjustment programs that are usually implemented in conjunction with devaluations.

Moreover, the exchange rate heavily affects the cost of external debt servicing which is crucial for less developed countries. In fact, large devaluations lead to exorbitant external debt servicing costs in terms of the local currency, which in turn lead to higher fiscal deficits and further inflationary pressures and exchange rate devaluations.

In theory, devaluation is an effective instrument to achieve balance of payments equilibrium, in that it stimulates exports and depresses the demand for imports. However, in a small, open economy like Somalia, whose main export is livestock, devaluation may only lead to higher import prices, higher inflation, and larger depreciation of the exchange rate. Furthermore, inflation undermines the functions of money, encourages short-term speculative activities at the expense of long-term productive investments, leads to social injustice, and breeds corruption that eats at the fabric of society and causes the disintegration of public institutions.

On the other hand, it should be observed that the exchange rate is not the culprit. Rather, it is an indicator that reflects past bad economic and financial policies. And in the case of Somalia, it reflects the extent to which the country had suffered from years of financial mismanagement, economic irrationality, civil war, anarchy, and destruction.

The question is: What is the appropriate exchange-rate regime to adopt in order to avoid currency crisis and confusion? There is no simple answer. As *The Economist* acknowledges, "emerging-market economies are confused about the right exchange-rate regime to pursue. Economists are confused too."[2] In general, there are two extreme types of exchange rate regimes: a freely floating regime where the exchange rate is determined by market forces, and a fixed regime kept fixed by the authorities. Between these two extremes, there is a wide range of intermediate arrangements that a country can adopt. The choice depends upon the particular circumstances of each country, for there is no one single exchange rate regime that is best for any one country all of the time and under all conditions.

In recommending a particular exchange rate system for a country, one has to take into account the characteristics of that country's economy. For a small, open country like Somalia, with rudimentary financial markets, a thin foreign exchange market, and a history of irresponsible monetary policy, the fixed exchange rate system is the most appropriate regime.[3] But a fixed exchange rate regime has to be supported by tough monetary and fiscal policies. If the authorities lack the credibility to enforce these policies, as happened in Somalia, a currency board system can best serve the interests of the country.

The currency board is a monetary authority that issues notes and coins in exchange for a reserve currency, e.g. the U.S. dollar. Unlike the central bank, the currency board cannot print money at will, since it is required to maintain foreign reserves equal in value to the total amount of notes and coins in circulation. The currency board system would help eliminate inflation, achieve exchange rate stability, impose financial discipline on the government, and above all reduce the scope for corruption and abuse of power by constraining the ability of government leaders to print money at their own discretion. It would also remove a source of conflict as rival factions and clans often fight over the control of sources of money supply.

To protect the currency board from political pressure, some form of foreign participation and supervision should be incorporated in its design. One must not underestimate the ability of Somali officials to circumvent the rule of law and/or operate outside the institutional framework.

---

[2]   "Spoilt for Choice." *The Economist* June 3, 2002.
[3]   "Getting Out of a Fix." *The Economist* September 20 1997.

Consider the former Central Bank of Somalia. According to its statutory law, the Bank was the authority legally responsible for the conduct of exchange rate policy with a clear mandate to specifically safeguard the external value of the Somali shilling.[4] Also, the Bank was statutorily responsible for the regulation of money and credit. In this respect, the Bank was prohibited from lending to the government more than 35 percent of the average actual revenues of the last three years. Needless to say, decisions regarding exchange rate policies or the regulation of money supply did not always rest with the Bank, but often were imposed on it in direct violation of the provision of the law. What is worse, the figures were sometimes manipulated in order to hide the full extent of the financial mismanagement.

Finally, one has to admit that the currency board system cannot fix all the monetary and financial problems of the country. At the end of the day, a currency is as strong as the country is. Obviously, if there is no peace, genuine reconciliation, and a responsible and functioning government, there can be no economic and financial development and the discussion of an exchange rate policy may be irrelevant.

The purpose of this book is to document the monetary and exchange rate policies and practices pursued in Somalia in the last thirty years, and look for lessons from past policy mistakes.

The book is organized in five chapters. The first chapter reviews some of the literature on the exchange rate determination. There are several theories explaining the rationale behind exchange rate movements. These will be briefly reviewed. The second chapter discusses the different exchange rate regimes from free-floating to rigidly fixed exchange rates to surrendering one's own national currency. It will also highlight the different exchange-rate regimes that existed in Somalia.

The third chapter traces the evolution of the problem of exchange rate instability in Somalia, looking into all the different phases through which the Somali shilling had gone over the years.

The fourth chapter analyzes data on money supply, inflation rates, and exchange movements. The analysis will concentrate on the relationship between growth in money supply on the one hand, and inflation and exchange rate depreciation on the other.

The fifth chapter offers recommendations for dealing with exchange rate stabilization. In particular, it proposes the introduction of the currency board system in Somalia as a means to stabilize the exchange rate.

---

4   Law No. 27 of 26 November 1968.

Finally, three appendices are provided at the end of the book: a list of senior managers of the Central Bank, chronology of major events that happened since 1991, and a glossary of economic terms.

I
DETERMINANTS OF
EXCHANGE RATES

Exchange rate movements are difficult to explain, as they are driven by many and complex forces. In this chapter, I will discuss the various approaches to exchange rate determination. It should be pointed from the outset that these approaches are not mutually exclusive. Each one explains the process of exchange rate determination from one perspective, and contributes to our understanding of this process.

Before we start, it may be useful to define some commonly used terms in exchange rate analysis:

Nominal exchange rate is here defined as the amount of domestic currency required to buy a unit of foreign currency. For example, when we say that one U.S. dollar is worth 20,000 Somali shillings, we are referring to the nominal exchange rate. When this amount rises, the nominal exchange rate is said to depreciate or weaken. When this amount falls, the currency is said to appreciate or strengthen. This is also called **direct quotation** as distinct from **indirect quotation,** which expresses the exchange rate as the number of units of the foreign currency needed to acquire one unit of domestic currency, example: 1 SoSh. is equal to 0.00005 U.S. dollars.

Real exchange rate is the nominal exchange rate adjusted for inflation differentials. For example, if prices in Somalia increase by 50 percent and 0 percent in U.S.A., and in the meantime, the shilling depreciates by 50 percent against the dollar, then the real exchange rate is unchanged.

Four approaches that explain the behavior of exchange rates are discussed below.

Purchasing Power Parity

The Purchasing Power Parity theory (PPP) explains the movements of the exchange rates in terms of inflation differentials. It states that, in equilibrium conditions, prices of the same goods and services in different countries must be equal when translated at the current exchange rate. Thus, the PPP exchange rate is the one that equates the price of externally traded goods in one country with the price of the same goods in another country.[5] In other words, if a country's inflation rate is higher than that of its trading partners, its exchange rate must depreciate in order to maintain its prices in line with those of its competitors. For example, if inflation in America is 6 percent and inflation in Canada is 4 percent, then the American dollar must fall by 2 percent to maintain the PPP.

The Economist magazine publishes every year what it calls the Big Mac index based on PPP theory. This says that the Big Mac sandwich, which is produced in 120 countries and has the same ingredients all over the world, should cost the same everywhere. But it doesn't. "Comparing actual exchange rates with Big Mac prices indicates whether a currency is under- or overvalued."[6]

The PPP suffers from a number of defects. First, it is difficult to establish a point at which currencies were in equilibrium. Second, there are many price indices, which do not only vary between themselves but also suffer from statistical defects and make the calculation of PPP very problematic. Third, many goods are not traded goods; that is, they are not imported or exported, which further complicates comparison between prices in different countries. Finally, PPP assumes a free flow of international trade. The reality is, however, different. In fact, there are innumerable barriers, tariffs, and other impediments that restrict world trade and cause distortions to price changes.

Researchers conclude that the PPP works relatively well when inflation differentials are large, e.g. when a country is in the throes of hyperinflation, and only over long periods of time. In the short run, exchange rate movements are driven by other factors, as we will see below[7].

---

[5]   Nick Douch, *The Economics of Foreign Exchange, A Practical Market Approach* (New York: Quorum Books). 1989.

[6]   *The Economist*, April 25, 2002.

[7]   Robert Lafrance and Simon van Norden, "Exchange rate fundamentals and the Canadian dollar," *Bank of Canada Review,* Spring 1995.

Balance of Payments Approach

The Balance of Payments Approach attributes movements in exchange rates to developments in the balance of payments. (For a definition of the balance of payments, see glossary.) According to this approach, the exchange rate is a price, and as such is determined by the demand for and supply of currencies in the foreign exchange market. As demand for foreign exchange is derived from imports, and the supply is derived from exports, the balance of payments is, therefore, regarded as a better indicator of exchange rate variations. Attention is focused on the current account, which comprises trade in goods, services, and transfers (grants and remittances). A deficit in the current account means that a country is paying for purchase of goods and services and for transfers more than it is obtaining. Such a deficit, the argument goes, will consequently lead to a depreciation of that country's currency. The opposite is true in the case of a surplus.

The role of the current account as a better guide for exchange rate movements is put into question. This is so because of the increasing importance of international capital movements, which are motivated by short-term interest rate differentials.

In fact, as a result of the generalized floating of exchange rates, the spread of technology, the globalization of markets, and the increased volatility of interest rates, funds move easily and quickly from one country to another, causing appreciation or depreciation even though the current account sends opposing signals.[8] For example, the U.S. dollar soared in foreign exchange markets for the last seven years, even though America recorded a huge current account deficit year after year ($430 billion in 2003 alone). In contrast, the Canadian dollar sank despite strong economic fundamentals. In the long run, however, the current account matters. Look again to the U.S. dollar. It started falling around the beginning of 2002, and has been steadily declining since then, as the huge U.S. current account deficit is not sustainable forever. There is even a fear of a coming dollar crush if the U.S. current account deficit is not cut.[9] On the other hand, the Canadian dollar soared to a ten-year high in October 2004, driven by strong economic fundamentals.[10]

---

[8] Charles N. Henning, William Pigott, Robert Haney Scott, *International Financial Management* (New York: McGraw Hill)

[9] C. Fred Bergsten. "The Risks Ahead for the World Economy." *The Economist,* September 9, 2004.

[10] *The Globe and Mail.* October 22, 2004.

Box 1. Balance of payments.

The balance of payments (BOP) records all transactions between the residents of one country and those of the rest of the world in a given period, usually a year. Any transaction that causes money to flow into the country is a credit and creates a supply of foreign exchange, and any transaction that causes money to flow out is a debit and generates a demand for foreign exchange. The BOP is divided into two main accounts: the current account, which comprises trade (imports and exports), services (transportation, travel), income (interest payments) and unilateral transfers (grants and remittances), and the capital & financial account, which measures the flow of investments and capital transfers.

To further illustrate the concept of the BOP, let us take the 1989 balance of payments of Somalia, the last published, as an example. As can be seen, in 1989, Somalia exported $67.7* million of goods and imported $346.3 million, thus recording a trade deficit of $278.6 million. There were also deficits on services ($122.0 million) and income ($84.4 million). However Somalia received grants amounting to $331.2 million, which reduced the deficit on the current account to $156.7 million. The capital account recorded a net outflow of $31.9 million (this could be payment of international loans or capital flight). Overall, the BOP showed a deficit of $189.4 million financed by international loans and reductions in foreign reserves. The balance of payments must always balance. A deficit is offset by a reduction in foreign reserves, and a surplus by an accumulation of foreign reserves. However, with a floating exchange rates regime, as is the case in Somalia, there are no deficits and surpluses. The floating exchange rate provides automatic balance of payments equilibrium.

Balance of Payments of Somalia: 1989 (in millions of U.S. dollars)

Current account balance	- 156.7
Exports	67.7
Imports	- 346.3
Trade balance	- 278.6
Services	- 122.0
Income	- 84.4
Unilateral transfers	331.2
Capital account	- 31.9
Statistical discrepancy	0.9
Overall balance	- 189.4

Source: International Financial Statistics Yearbook, IMF, Washington 1992

* Exports were often under-invoiced, which explains why the figure is so low.

The Balance of Payments approach emphasizes the importance of economic fundamentals in determining the level of real exchange rates. Examples of such economic fundamentals might be changes in productivity, level of income, change in world prices of domestic goods, discovery of natural resources, trade restraints, relative preferences for domestic versus foreign goods, etc. Imagine what would happen to the exchange rate of the Somali shilling if miraculously one day, people in Somalia stop chewing Qat (a mild stimulant narcotic chewed like tobacco).[11]

The Balance of Payments approach may be valid over the long-term period, but in the short and medium-term, it also fails to explain the movement of exchange rates.

The Asset Market Approach

Today's foreign exchange markets are dominated by a multitude of investors and speculators who are motivated by profit-making or risk-avoiding. By transferring funds quickly and massively from one currency to another, these investors/speculators cause sharp swings in exchange rates that are not often justified by balance of payments developments or other economic fundamentals.

The Asset Market Approach attempts to explain why exchange rates fluctuate more than is warranted by economic fundamentals. According to this approach, currencies are considered as assets such as stocks and bonds. As any other assets, demand for currencies is determined by the investors/speculators. It follows that expectations of future events, be they political, economic, or even trivial, will affect the exchange rate. It is estimated that more than U.S. \$1.2 trillion worth of currencies are traded each day in the foreign exchange market.[12]

The Monetary Approach to Exchange Rates

The Monetary Approach to exchange rates views the process of exchange determination as a monetary phenomenon. It focuses on the demand for and supply of monetary assets. This approach postulates that

---

[11]   In September 1999, the Kenyan government imposed a ban on all flights to and from Somalia. The ban affected Qat imports and as a result, the Somali shilling appreciated from SoSh. 10,150 to SoSh. 9,900 per dollar in few days. *Xinhua* Sept. 2, 1999.

[12]   Bank for International Settlements (2001) Triennial Central Bank Survey of Foreign Exchange and Derivatives Marker Activity. Basle

since the exchange rate is the price of one currency in terms of another currency, then it must be determined by the relative supply of and demand for the two currencies. For example, if money supply grows faster in one country than in the rest of the world, while demand for money remains the same, the exchange rate of the country experiencing higher growth of money supply should depreciate.

The Monetary Approach to exchange rates assumes that the Purchasing Power Parity holds true, that money supply is controlled by the Central Bank, and that relative interest rates affect the demand for money.[13]

In its simplest form, the Monetary Approach to Exchange Rates states that an excess money supply will lead to an increase in prices, which in turn will cause a depreciation of the currency or a deterioration of the balance of payments.

The simple monetary model is said to be an extreme case not very close to developments in the real world.[14] It also has been criticized for failing to provide "an adequate explanation of the movements in major currency values during the floating rate period that began in 1973".[15] Furthermore, some economists rejected what they called the strong version of the Monetary Approach, which always identifies balance of payments deficits with an excess money supply. Instead, they suggested a weak version that reconciles with other approaches, and recognizes that "although shifts in the demand for and supply of money to hold are not necessarily the immediate cause of exchange rate movements, they can be and perhaps usually are".[16]

Exchange Rate Determination in Somalia

In this section, I will attempt to explain the rationale behind the movements of exchange rates in Somalia. In analyzing the causes of exchange rate depreciation in Somalia, I will argue that the weak version of the monetary approach applies. At the same time, I acknowledge the

---

[13] Nick Douch, *The Economics of Foreign Exchange,* op. cit.

[14] Edward Sebastian, "Exchange Rate Misalignment in Developing Countries," *World Bank Occasional Paper No. 2,* new series, John Hopkins University Press.

[15] James M. Bougton, "The Monetary Approach to Exchange Rates: What Remains?" *Essays in International Finance No. 171,* Princeton University, Princeton, New Jersey.

[16] Alan A. Rabin and Leland B. Yeager, "Monetary Approach to Balance of Payments and Exchange Rates", *Essays in International Finance No. 148,* Nov. 1982, Princeton University, Princeton, New Jersey.

importance of other factors. Indeed, balance of payments developments, expectations, and political uncertainties have played their part. But the point is that without monetary accommodation, the effects of the other factors would have been absorbed or even reversed. In my view, the Monetary Approach is relevant in the case of Somalia, because of the following reasons:

1. Excessive monetary creation had been going on for quite a long time to dissipate in the minds of the public any sort of money illusion. This means that changes in money supply would not affect output but would only fuel inflation.

2. The massive growth in money supply during the 1980s and 1990s, and the consequent high inflation rates and perennial exchange rate depreciations, brought about a widespread "dollarization" of the economy as people learned to switch shillings into dollars as a hedge against inflation. After 1991, the "dollarization" phenomenon increased to such an extent that the dollar is now used not only as a store of value but also as the most preferred means of payment. In addition, the parallel market became now the only foreign exchange market where the Somali shilling floats freely with full convertibility. Under these conditions, any excess monetary creation affects immediately the exchange rate, causing a chain reaction of depreciation-inflation-depreciation, as demonstrated by the experience of the shilling in the 1980s, and especially the reaction of the exchange rate to the injection of cash in the form of fake banknote by faction leaders and businessmen in the late 1990s. A likely scenario will be as follows: excess money is created, Somali shillings are converted into dollars, the exchange rate depreciates, merchants revise the prices of their stocks upward as they anticipate higher import costs in terms of the local currency, the general level of prices rises sharply, further depreciation follows, and the process goes on. On the other hand, if new money is not created, inflation absorbs the excess liquidity from the market and causes the exchange rate to stabilize and strengthen over time, as happened in the first part of the 1990s.

From the Balance of Payments point of view, the exchange rate is dominated by a few key items, notably livestock exports estimated at U.S. $200 million annually and remittances estimated at U.S. $750 million to

U.S. $1 billion a year[17]. Qat imports conservatively estimated at $150,000 per day represent the single largest item consuming foreign exchange resources and a serious drain of hard currency out of Somalia.[18]

---

[17]   "Report on Supporting Systems and Procedures for the Effective Regulation and Monitoring of Somali Remittance Companies", UNDP 2003

[18]   UNDP Somalia (1998) Human Development Report, Nairobi.

II
EXCHANGE RATE REGIMES

In this chapter, I will examine the different exchange rate regimes, which basically deal with the mechanism of setting the exchange rates. There is a wide range of exchange rate arrangements, from free floating to permanent fixing, or even surrendering one's own national currency. All these regimes will be discussed.

Floating Exchange Rates

Free Float

Exchange rates are said to be freely floating when they are determined by the forces of demand and supply without government intervention.

Supporters of floating exchange rates argue that such a system is advantageous because it provides a continuous and smooth adjustment of the exchange rate, relieves the authorities from holding large foreign exchange reserves to support their currencies, and depoliticizes the process of exchange rate setting. They also argue that floating exchange rates help cushion the effects of economic shocks. For example, if the world price of a key export commodity falls, the exchange rate depreciates as a result, and reduces the negative impact on exporters.

The chief disadvantage of this system is that movements in exchange rates can be large and frequent and to a level not warranted by economic fundamentals. These disorderly fluctuations in the exchange rate may cause uncertainty in international trade, make business planning and pricing difficult, and harm productivity and economic growth. Free float is not recommended for small, developing countries with thin foreign exchange markets, rudimentary money and capital markets, substantial foreign exchange liabilities, and weak currencies. Usually, their exchange rates sink instead of floating, causing significant disruption of the economy.

Free or "clean" floating is seldom encountered in real world (present stateless Somalia being the exception). Instead, "dirty" or managed floating is the norm. This is so because exchange rates are so pervasive in their effect that governments feel obliged to intervene, from time to time, in the foreign exchange market to prevent sharp fluctuations of their currencies.

Managed float

Under managed floating, the central bank intervenes in the foreign exchange market only to smooth out short-term fluctuations. The problem is that the central bank may not know whether it is dealing with short-term fluctuations or with a fundamental trend.

Partial floating

This system is mainly practiced in developing countries. It is characterized by the existence of two markets: A free market, in which the exchange rate is determined by the interplay of market forces, and an official market, controlled by the government. Under this system, exporters and other foreign exchange earners are allowed to retain a portion of their foreign exchange income and sell it in the parallel market at market-determined rates.

The advantage of this system is that it reduces the scope for illegal black market, and allows the government time to unify the two markets. Its chief disadvantage is that it discourages those exports which are channeled through the official market, and may encourage the illegal siphoning off of resources from the official to the free market where the exchange rate is high.

Auction

Under this system, foreign exchange is auctioned to successful bidders. Supply of foreign exchange comes from specified exports, services, and transfers which are surrendered to the central bank and auctioned on regular basis (fortnightly, weekly, or even daily). All bidders are required to lodge either partial or equivalent of 100 percent of the foreign exchange they are going to purchase. Once bids are opened and examined, foreign exchange is allocated to the successful bidders from the highest bidder to the bid, which exhausts the available supply and clears the market. This rate becomes the market exchange rate and applies until the next auction. Under a "Dutch auction" system, each bidder pays his bid price, and the weighted average bid price may determine the exchange rate.[19]

Interbank

Under this system, the exchange rate is determined in negotiations between the central bank and the commercial banks on the basis of the demand for and supply of foreign exchange. Individuals and firms bid through the commercial banks.

Fixed Exchange Rates

Under this system, exchange rates are determined by the authorities, which accept an obligation to peg the exchange rate at a determined level and prevents the market deviating from that level. The exchange rate may be fixed against one important international currency, such as the U.S. dollar, or against a basket of currencies.

Supporters of fixed exchange system argue that it provides a high degree of stability and thereby promotes investment and international trade. It also imposes monetary discipline by fixing the national currency to that of a country with a sound currency. The fixed exchange rate system is criticized for being too inflexible and vulnerable to speculative attacks that ultimately force its abandonment.

Crawling peg

Under this system, the exchange rate is adjusted gradually according to a schedule. For example, the exchange rate may be devalued by 0.25 percent every month in order to offset inflation differentials.

---

[19] Peter J. Quirk, Benedicte Vibe Christensen, Kyung-Mo Huh, and Toshiko Sasaki, Floating Exchange Rates in Developing Countries, Experience with Auction and Interbank Markets, IMF, Washington, D.C. May 1987

Fixed But Adjustable

Under this system, the exchange rate is fixed but not guaranteed ("soft peg"). Analysts contend that "soft pegs" cannot only be sustained but contribute to financial crises in developing countries.[20] The problem arises when a government under this system pursues deficit-financing policies. The expanding money supply associated with the deficit financing leads eventually to balance of payments deterioration, loss of reserves, and build-up of speculation. At the end, the government will be forced to devalue in an environment of economic crisis and political recrimination.

Currency Board

The currency board arrangement is a very rigid form of fixed exchange rates ("hard peg"). Under this system, the exchange rate is fixed against a reserve currency, usually the U.S. dollar at a specified rate written into law. Moreover, the domestic currency is fully convertible and is 100 percent backed by foreign reserves equal in value to the total amount of notes and coins in circulation.

Advocates of the currency board system argue that it provides price stability, a stable exchange rate, and currency convertibility, which result from the imposition of strict fiscal discipline.   The resulting stable economic environment promotes trade, investment, and economic growth. The currency board is also praised because of its simplicity, transparency, and ease of implementation.

The currency board system is criticized for being inflexible and not allowing the use of discretionary monetary policies to suit a country's own economic conditions. In fact, the amount of money in circulation is not controlled by the central bank, but automatically determined by changes in the balance of payments. For example, a deficit in the balance of payments creates an outflow of foreign reserves, which causes the currency in circulation to contract, and hence the interest rate to rise sharply, leading to unemployment and economic stagnation.

Another weakness of the currency board system is that it precludes use of the exchange rate as an instrument for correcting balance of payments imbalances. As the local currency is linked to a strong currency, it could become overvalued and make the country's exports uncompetitive. This is what happened to Argentina. The rising U.S. dollar in the latter part of the 1990s forced the peso to move upward with it and made Argentina's exports

---

[20]   UNCTAD, Trade and Development Report, page 111.

very expensive in international markets, throwing the country into recession. By locking itself into a rigid fixed exchange system, Argentina could not lower interest rates to stimulate the economy or restore competitiveness by letting the exchange rate to depreciate. The situation was made worse by the fact that Brazil, Argentina's largest trading partner, devalued significantly its currency, gaining a competitive trade advantage over Argentina. At the end, Argentina had to abandon the currency board after weeks of political and social unrest that toppled the government.

The turmoil in Argentina has raised serious concerns about the currency board system. Was it a policy mistake for Argentina to adopt the system? Opinions are divided. Some economists blame the currency board, others argue that Argentina was badly mistaken to cling to the currency board arrangement for so long, while still others focus on Argentina's unique problems, which included a high external debt, large budget deficits, intransigent unions, and obsolete industries[21]. Hong Kong, Bulgaria, Bosnia, Estonia, and many other countries still use and support the currency board arrangement.

According to John Williamson, Senior Fellow at the Institute for International Economics, the currency board system is superior in situations when the country is small, open to international trade, and there is a total collapse of confidence in the domestic currency.[22]

Dollarization

There are three stages of dollarization:
1. Official dollarization, or full dollarization, occurs when a country gives up its own currency and adopts a foreign currency, most often the U.S. dollar as a legal tender and means of payment for all transactions.
2. Semiofficial dollarization occurs when a country uses a foreign currency as legal tender alongside the local currency.
3. Unofficial dollarization occurs when citizens of a country use the foreign currency as a store of value.[23]

---

[21] "Dollar Mad?" *The Economist.* October 25, 2001.

[22] John Williamson, "What Role for Currency Boards?" *Institute For International Economics,* September 1995.

[23] Michael J. Lambert and Kristin D. Stanton, "Opportunities and Challenges of the U.S. Dollar as an Increasingly Global Currency." *Federal Reserve Bulletin,* September 2001.

As may be noted, the term "dollarization" applies to the use of any foreign currency by another country. Examples of countries using the U.S. dollar as legal tender include Panama, Ecuador, El Salvador, and Guatemala. Lesotho and Swaziland use the South African rand. Some Eastern European countries are contemplating the adoption of the euro.

Advocates of dollarization maintain that a dollarizing country will replace its less stable domestic currency with a stable world currency, e.g., the U.S. dollar and, as a result, will enjoy a lower interest rate, lower inflation, higher investment, and faster economic growth. But dollarization has also its costs. A dollarizing country forgoes seigniorage revenue, or the profit that accrues to a government that issues currency. Also, a dollarizing country will forfeit its monetary autonomy to a foreign country and will constrain its ability to use discretionary monetary policies to deal with macroeconomic problems.

Opponents of dollarization point out that there is no evidence that dollarization by itself leads to fiscal prudence, or the elimination of a country's risk, or better balance of payments performance. According to one economist "the recent push for dollarization is a typical case of misleading advertisement." [24]

Dollarization is a "hard peg" like the currency board. And as such is appropriate only for small countries that are integrated into the economy of the country whose currency they use and under extreme financial instability. Compared to dollarization, the currency board may be preferable. With a currency board, a country can retain its national currency and earn substantial seigniorage revenue.

Currency Union

The turmoil in the foreign exchange markets and the successful introduction of the euro generated considerable interest in currency unions as a means to achieve exchange rate stability as well as regional economic integration. For example, the members of the Economic Community of West African States (ECOWAS) have agreed to adopt a common currency by the year 2003.[25] Likewise, the members of the Cooperation Council of the Arab States of the Gulf (GCC) have decided to launch by January 1,

---

[24] Sebastian Edwards, "The false promise of dollarization," *Financial Times,* May 10, 2001.

[25] The six countries are: Ghana, Nigeria, Liberia, Sierra Leone, Gambia and Guinea.

2010, a monetary union with a single currency pegged to the U.S. dollar.[26] Also, there have been some discussions of an eventual currency union among the Association of Southeast Asian Nations (ASEAN) plus China and Japan.[27] Proposals for a common currency in North America and in Latin America have been floated from time to time.

At present, there are few common currency areas in developing countries. One such area is the Communaute Financiere Africaine or the African Financial Community (CFA) which shares a common currency the CFA franc. The CFA community comprises fourteen countries in West and Central Africa, twelve of which are former French colonies. The countries are organized into two regional groupings. Eight countries— Benin, Burkina Faso, Cote d'Ivoire, Guinea-Bissau, Mali, Niger, Senegal, and Togo—form the West African Economic and Monetary Union (WAEMU), while six countries—Cameroon, Central African Republic, Chad, Republic of Congo, Equatorial Guinea, and Gabon—form the Central African Economic and Monetary Community (BEAC). The CFA franc was pegged to the French franc until 2002, when the CFA franc was tied to the euro. The French Treasury guarantees the convertibility of the CFA franc.[28]

Another common currency area is shared by the Organization of Eastern Caribbean States (OECS) with comprises eight small island economies: Antigua and Barbuda, Dominica, Grenada, St. Kitts and Nevis, St. Lucia, St. Vincent and the Grenadines, Anguilla, and Montserrat. The OECS members share a common currency, the Eastern Caribbean dollar, which is pegged to the U.S. dollar.[29]

A common currency brings a number of economic benefits to the participating countries. It eliminates the costs of conversion from one currency to another, reduces the risk of exchange rate fluctuations, spurs greater competition and efficiency, and promotes trade among the partner countries. Increased efficiency and economies of scale should lower prices and raise the standard of living of the citizens of participating countries. The conversion to a single currency brings also some costs. The main

---

[26]   BBC News, Business. 2 January 2003. The six members of GCC are Bahrain, Kuwait, Oman, Qatar, Saudi Arabia, and the United Arab Emirates.

[27]   The countries are: Brunei, Indonesia, Malaysia, Philippines, Singapore, Thailand, Cambodia, Laos, Burma, and Vietnam.

[28]   From *Africa Recovery*, Vol. 12 #4 (April 1999).

[29]   Frits van Beek, Jose Roberto Rosales, Mayra Zermeno, Ruby Randall, and Jorge Shepard. "The East Caribbean Currency Union. Institutions, Performance and Policy Issues." IMF (2000).

disadvantage is the loss of economic flexibility and inability to use the exchange rates to buffer economic shocks that affect partner countries at different times and to different degrees.

To have a successful currency union, the participating countries must coordinate their monetary and economic policies. Also, there should be greater worker and capital mobility and transfer of resources among national economies.

The mere creation of a currency union does not diminish the challenge faced by developing countries as to what currency regime to adopt or how to achieve exchange rate stability. In addition, developing countries may find it very difficult to sustain a currency union without the involvement of a major reserve currency country.[30]

Exchange control

Exchange controls are usually practiced under fixed exchange rate regimes. Under this system, the authorities require that all citizens who acquire foreign exchange surrender the foreign money to the authorities, and all those who need foreign exchange apply to the authorities for authorization. The domestic currency is thus, inconvertible. In the past, less developed countries used to impose this type of controls in order to ration scarce foreign exchange resources among various users.

Exchange controls are criticized on the grounds that they have limited success, deter capital inflows, and create black markets and incentives for fraud.

Few countries nowadays practice foreign exchange controls and only in respect to capital outflows aimed at preventing speculative attacks on the exchange rate.

Exchange Rate Regimes of Somalia.

Almost all sorts of exchange rate regimes have been experimented with in Somalia as enumerated here below:
- *Exchange control system:* This system was in effect throughout the period 1960-1990.
- *Flexible exchange rates system:* This system was used during 1960-1971 under the Bretton Woods arrangement of fixed but

---

[30] UNCTAD, op. cit.
[31] Bretton Woods is a locality in New Hampshire, USA where the international conference establishing the IMF and the World Bank was held.

adjustable rates.[31]

- *Partial floating:* This system was used during the period 1976-1990; that is when the "Franco Valuta" system (the parallel market) was introduced.

- *Crawling peg:* This system was used in 1986. During that period, the official rate used to be adjusted on a weekly basis for inflation differentials between the Somali shilling and a basket of currencies representing Somalia's major trading partners.

- *Auction system:* The auction system was used during the period 1986-1990.

- *Managed floating:* This system was used during the period 1986-1990, which coincides with the auction system. In fact, the auction system represented a managed floating system, since the Central Bank made interventions in the foreign exchange market.

- *Free floating:* This system is in effect from 1991 to the present, or since the collapse of the Somali government.

- *Dollarization:* Semi-official dollarization is in effect since 1991, as the dollar is used as means of payment along side the Somali shilling.

One may wonder why the exchange rate system of Somalia was so unsuccessful. The problem, however, is not with the exchange-rate regime, but rather with the fiscal and monetary policies. In fact, "no exchange rate system can do well if fiscal and monetary policies are out of control, while most exchange systems will do reasonably well if fiscal and monetary policies are prudent."[32] Or as the former governor of the Bank of Canada put it: "No exchange-rate system is going to bail you out of bad economic policies. This is equally true of a floating exchange-rate system, as it is of the alternatives—a fixed exchange rate or indeed a monetary union, even if that monetary union is with the world's largest, strongest economy."[33]

What exchange-rate regime is appropriate for Somalia? There is no such thing as a perfect exchange-rate regime. The fixed exchange-

---

[32] Carlos Diaz-Alejandro. A comment, in *Economic Adjustment and Exchange Rates in Developing Countries,* edited by Sebastian Edwards and Liaqat Ahmed, The University of Chicago Press, 1986 p.418.

[33] Gordon Thiessen, "The Conduct of Monetary Policy When You Live Next Door to a Large Neighbor." *World Economic Affaires,* Volume 3 No. 2 Autumn 2000.

rate system may be appropriate under some conditions and the flexible exchange rates under others. The option depends upon the particular circumstances of each country. Experience teaches us that there is no one single exchange rate arrangement that is good for any one country all of the time. Therefore, in recommending an exchange rate system for Somalia, I consider the following characteristics of the Somali economy:

- the small size of the economy;
- the openness of the economy to foreign trade;
- the dependence on the export of few primary products. For example, livestock exports and livestock products account for more than 80 percent of total foreign exchange earnings;
- the history of currency crisis, monetary disorder and financial chaos that plagued the country in the last twenty-five years;
- the lack of institutions and expertise to conduct an independent monetary policy;
- the political culture in Somalia where the state is perceived as a source of easy money and the fact that the notion of financial accountability is almost nonexistent;
- the lack of a banking system, with the economy being entirely cash-based;
- the extensive dollarization of the economy, the U.S. dollar being the predominant currency in circulation in Somalia;
- the lack of financial and economic data, with the exchange rate being the only readily available economic indicator.

In the light of these considerations, I recommend the adoption of a fixed exchange rate system in Somalia by means of a currency board mechanism and consider such a system to be the best option for Somalia. Section five discusses how to operate the currency board in more detail.

III
THE EVOLUTION OF THE EXCHANGE RATE PROBLEM IN SOMALIA

Historical Background.

During the Second World War, Britain occupied the southern part of Somalia, which was until then an Italian colony. The northern part of Somalia was, and remained, a British protectorate. During that period, the British administration introduced the East African shilling to Somalia. The latter circulated in Kenya, Uganda, and Tanganyika. The East African shilling (E.A.Sh.) was issued by the East African Currency Board, based in London until 1960, and had a gold parity of .0124414 grams, which was equivalent to an exchange rate of E.A.Sh. 7.14 per U.S. dollar or E.A.Sh. 20 per UK pound. In 1960, the East African Currency Board was transferred from London to Nairobi, Kenya.

In 1950, the southern part of Somalia was transferred to Italian Trusteeship Administration under United Nations supervision. The Italian Administration followed the example of the British. They introduced a currency board, "Cassa per la Circolazione Monetaria della Somalia (CCMS)" and issued a new currency called "Somalo", which had the same gold parity as the E.A.Sh. and the same denominations, namely 5-, 10-, 20-, and 100-shilling banknotes; and 1.00 Somalo; 50-, 10-, 5- and 1-cent coins.[34]

---

[34] Somali National Bank, Annual Report, 1960, Mogadishu, 1961.

On July 1, 1960, Italian Somalia and British Somaliland, after attaining independence, united to form the Republic of Somalia. On the same day, the Somali National Bank was established and the currency was renamed as the Somali shilling (SoSh.), with a gold parity of .0124414 grams or SoSh. 7.14 per U.S. dollar, the same as the E.A.Sh. and the Somalo, and with full backing of foreign reserves.[35]

In 1966, the exchange control system was reformed. Restrictions on imports were relaxed. An advisory committee consisting of members from the Central Bank and the ministry of trade was established to authorize payments of foreign exchange for services, mainly travel.

In 1968, a new Central Bank Law was enacted. At the same time, the requirement of covering the currency in circulation with foreign reserves and gold was abolished. Instead, restrictions were imposed on the government's borrowing from the Central Bank.

In October 1969, General Mohamed Siad Barre seized power in a military coup. One year later, the military regime declared Scientific Socialism and nationalized all major economic activities. Of particular importance was the nationalization of four foreign- owned commercial banks, namely Banco di Roma, Banco di Napoli, National and Grindlays Bank, and Banque de Port Said.

Five-shilling East African Currency Board

---

[35]   The Somali National Bank inherited foreign reserves and gold worth U.S. $6 million backing the amount of notes in circulation as of June 30, 1960.

Twenty-Somalo notes issued by CC MS in 1950

Twenty-shilling note introduced by Banca Nazionale Somala in 1962 replacing CCMS notes

100-shilling note issued by Bankiga Qaranka Soomaaliyed (Somali National Bank) in 1975

500-shilling note issued by Bankiga Dhexe ee Soomaaliya (Central Bank of Somalia) in 1989

1,000-shilling note introduced in 1990 and reprinted over again and again by the Warlords

Fifty-shilling "N" currency introduced by Ali Mahdi in 1991

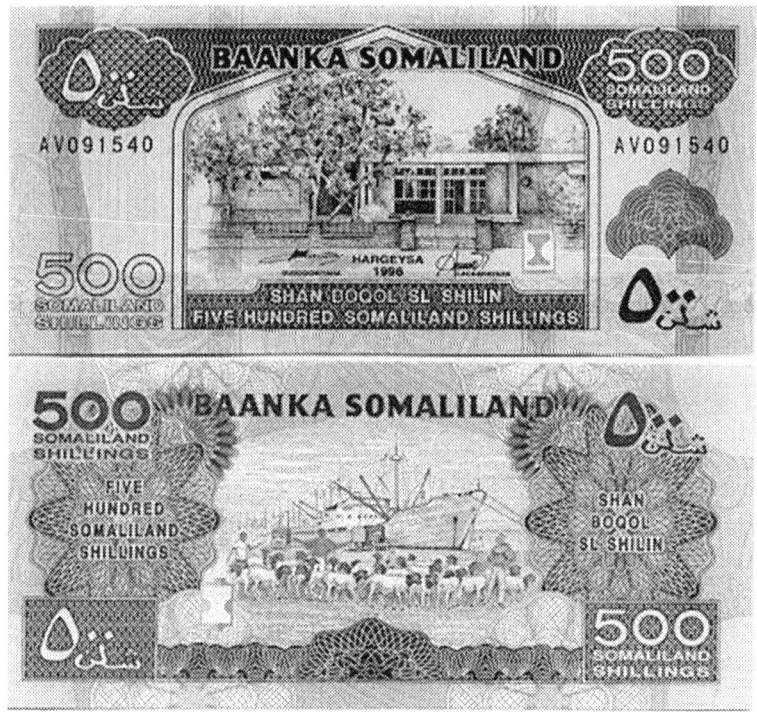

500 Somaliland shilling banknote printed in 1996

100 Somaliland banknote issued in 1996

Box 2. Functions of Money

Money serves three important functions in the economy:

Medium of Exchange or Means of Payment: We use money in exchange for the goods and services we need in our daily life. As a means of payment, money facilitates the transactions and makes economic exchanges easier and more efficient. Without money, there is no specialization, and therefore no economic efficiency. As it is said, money "greases the wheel of the economy."

Unit of Account or Standard of Value: Money is used as a yardstick, a standard by which the prices of all other goods and services are expressed. Just as distance is measured in kilometers, the value of goods is measured in shillings, dollars, pounds, dinars, etc.

Store of Value or Wealth: Money provides us with a convenient way to save a portion of our wealth in an easily spendable form for our future needs.

To serve these functions, money must possess certain characteristics. It must be widely acceptable to people as a means of payment. It must also be divisible to allow you to buy the item you want to purchase and get your change. It must also be portable; that is, not too heavy to carry around. And finally money must be stable in value. This is possible if the supply of commodity used as money is controlled, otherwise inflation will occur and money will cease to function as a store of value and eventually as a unit of account and means of payment.

How does the Somali shilling perform the above-mentioned functions? As a store of value, the shilling lost its role long time ago in the early 1980s as a result of the high inflation rate and the ensuing large and continuous devaluations. The U.S. dollar replaced the Somali shilling in that respect. The dollar is also predominantly used as a unit of account and means of payment. The shilling maintains precariously some of its usefulness as a medium of exchange, especially with respect to small-value transactions. It is mainly used by the small-scale traders and by the rural population. While the problem of the shilling is portability (too bulky to carry around because of the inflation), the problem with the U.S. dollar is divisibility (indivisible for small value transactions).

Out of the nationalized banks came two new government-owned banks, the Somali Commercial Bank and the Somali Savings and Credit Bank.

In 1975, a mini reorganization of the banking system was carried out. The two banks were amalgamated into one bank, the Commercial and Savings Bank of Somalia (CSBS), which remained the only commercial bank in the country until it collapsed in 1990 and dragged the whole financial system down. Furthermore, the Somali National Bank's name was changed to Central Bank of Somalia.

In 1989, a new banking law was enacted with technical assistance from the IMF. The law authorized the establishment of private banks in Somalia.

In January 1991, Siad Barre was ousted from power and forced to flee from the capital. Since then, Somalia had no central government and no national monetary authority.

From 1991, some faction leaders, regional administrators, and businessmen started printing new Somali shilling banknotes. The first faction leader to import currency was Ali Mahdi, the former North Mogadishu leader who introduced a new currency, the "N" currency, which was ordered by the former government as part of its stabilization policy and was to replace the notes used up to 1990. In fact, "N" means a new shilling and is equal to 100 old Somali shillings. The "N" currency's circulation is limited to North Mogadishu.

In 1994, The Somaliland administration introduced the Somaliland shilling which circulates in western and parts of eastern Somaliland.

In 1996, Mohamed Farah Aideed entered into a deal with a Canadian company, the British American Banknote Company, based in Ottawa, Canada, and a Malaysian intermediary, Adorna Group of Malaysia, to print a massive amount of banknotes worth SoSh. 165 billion.[36] The first shipment, worth SoSh. 32.5, was received by Hussein Aideed in 1996. The balance was imported, in four successive batches, by businessmen of Aideed's kin.

In 1999, the Puntland administration started printing banknotes to claim its share of the windfall seigniorage revenue. The notes were printed in Indonesia.

---

[36]   *National Post,* Ottawa. June 23, 1999.

In 2000 and 2001, businessmen flooded the market with fake banknotes, with devastating effects on the economy and the lives of the people, especially the poor.[37]

In June 2003, Abdinur Darman, a Mogadishu businessman of Aideed's kin, declared himself president of Somalia on Al-Jazeera TV. He then traveled to Malaysia to import a   consignment of fake banknotes he ordered in 1997, which remained stockpiled in Malaysia in the possession of the printer.[38]

---

[37] Technically, the banknotes printed by the factions cannot be called counterfeit, since there is no legitimate Somali government. For example, Canada's Foreign Affairs Department urged the British American Company to stop printing the fake Somali currency. However, its warnings were unheeded by the company, as there was no legal basis on which the Canadian government could prevent the transaction from taking place. Source: *National Post,* Ottawa, June 23, 1999.

[38] Report of Panel of Experts on Somalia Pursuant to the Security Council resolution 1474(2003).

Box 3. Currencies of Somalia, a Timeline[39]

1800s	Before the arrival of the colonial powers, the Maria Theresa Thaler circulated in Somalia. This was a silver coin minted in Austria from 1740 to 1780 which became very popular in some parts of Africa and Arabia.
1884	Britain reintroduced the Indian rupee in British Protectorate of Somaliland. The Indian rupee circulated in the area along with Maria Theresa before the arrival of the British.
1909	Italy introduced the rupia to Italian Somalia. This was a silver coin divisible in 100 bese.
1925	Italy introduced the Italian lira to Italian Somalia and established a branch of Banca d'Italia in Mogadishu.
1936	Somalia becomes part of the Italian East Africa. The Italian lira, Serie Africa Orientale was introduced.
1941	Britain introduced the East African shilling to British Somaliland and former Italian Somalia.
1950	Italian Trusteeship Administration introduced the Somalo at bar with the East African shilling.
1960	Somali Republic introduced the Somali shilling. The Somalo replaced the East African shilling in the northern region.
1962	New Somali shilling notes were introduced, replacing the Somalo, which ceased to be legal tender in December 1963.
1967	New Somali shilling coins were introduced, replacing the Somalo coins.
1989	New 500-shilling banknote was introduced.
1990	New 1,000-shilling note was introduced.
1991	Ali Mahdi introduced the "N" currency.
1994	Somaliland introduced the Somaliland shilling.
1996	From 1996, faction leaders start introducing fake currency by reprinting the 1,000-Somali shilling banknote.

---

[39] Some of the information was sourced from: "A global history of currencies." www.globalfindata.com.

The Years of Stability 1960-1970

During the 1960s, the SoSh. displayed a remarkable degree of stability. The official rate remained fixed at its declared gold parity (SoSh. 7.14 per U.S. dollar) and the country adhered firmly to the fixed exchange rate system. Under such a system, countries could devalue or revalue their currencies only under conditions of "fundamental disequilibrium" and with the consent of the International Monetary Fund (IMF).[40]

The stability of the SoSh. can be better gauged by the absence of a parallel market rate of any significance, and the reduced level of restrictiveness of the exchange control system during the period under review. Nevertheless, economic conditions were not without strains. In 1964, a severe balance of payments situation emerged. An overall deficit of SoSh. 60 million was recorded in 1964, and the trade deficit reached an all-time high of So.Sh. 202 million. In 1965, net foreign reserves dropped to an uncomfortably low level of So.Sh. 5.8 million. Several factors were responsible for the strained balance of payments conditions. In early 1964, there was a border clash with Ethiopia, drought had struck in many parts of the country, and the United Kingdom terminated its aid to Somalia following a breakup of diplomatic relations between the two countries.[41]

In 1965, the authorities adopted a comprehensive stabilization program under a standby arrangement from the International Monetary Fund. The program relied on credit control as an instrument of stabilization, which proved very successful. So successful was the program that a 1971-73 development plan document had to note: "The economic picture, as the 1971-73 plan gets underway, is reasonably bright, consumer prices are stable, the trade deficit is improving, and the government's budget for this year is in balance. The national foreign exchange reserves are at a ten year high."[42]

The Pegging of the Somali Shilling

In 1971, the U.S. dollar crisis disturbed the international monetary system and caused the collapse of the fixed exchange-rate system. On August 15, 1971, the U.S. government suspended the convertibility of the

---

[40] Robert Solomon, *The International Monetary System, 1945-1981: An insider's view.* (New York: Harper and Row, 1982).

[41] Somali National Bank, Annual Reports, various issues.

[42] Somali Democratic Republic, Ministry of National Planning, Three-Year Plan 1971-73, Mogadishu 1971.

U.S. dollar into gold and devalued the dollar, establishing a new parity of U.S. $38 per ounce of fine gold. Many countries followed the example of the U.S. government and devalued their currencies. Somalia, however, did not devalue and the new SoSh/U.S.$ exchange rate became SoSh. 6.91 per U.S. dollar. On June 23, 1972, the British authorities decided to float the pound sterling. The floating of the pound sterling and its continued deterioration caused many difficulties to the Somali exporters, because the pound was the major export currency, particularly for the livestock sector. To cope with this problem, the Central Bank of Somalia introduced a system of differentiated spreads between buying and selling rates ranging from 2.3 to 4.5 percent.

In 1973, international foreign exchange markets experienced unrest. The U.S. dollar was further devalued, and finally the Bretton Woods system broke down, and was replaced by a floating exchange rate system.[43] Again, Somalia did not deem it necessary to follow the U.S. dollar devaluation, and therefore the SoSh./U.S.$ rate appreciated to SoSh. 6.29 per U.S. dollar.

The advent of the generalized floating system confronted the Somali authorities with a new problem: how to set the value of SoSh. against other currencies in a regime of floating exchange rates. After some initial hesitation, the Somali authorities decided to peg the SoSh. to the U.S. dollar, instructed exporters to switch their earning currencies from the UK pound and Italian lira to the U.S. dollar, and unified the spreads between the buying and selling rates to 2 percent. The peg to the U.S. dollar was justified, because many developing countries, some of which Somalia had close trade relations with—such as Saudi Arabia and Kenya—had switched to the U.S. dollar.

The peg at the rate of SoSh. 6.29 per U.S. dollar remained unchanged for a long time, 1973-1981. That, however, did not mean true stability, as we will see in the following section.

The Emergence of the Parallel Exchange Market 1971-1980

The origins of the parallel exchange market lie in the nationalization policies adopted by the Somali government in the 1970s. Between 1970 and 1975, the government nationalized the importation of foodstuffs, petroleum products, construction materials, medicines and pharmaceuticals, clothes, and a wide range of other commodities. By October 1975, all import trade

---

[43]   Robert Solomon. Op. Cit.

was practically under state monopoly with twelve government agencies involved in foreign trade.

State trading proved disastrous in terms of the balance of payments position. Lack of experience in foreign trade, poor distribution and inventory systems, combined with waste, mismanagement, and patronage, caused an upsurge in imports and shifted the balance of payments from a surplus of SoSh. 124 million in 1972 to deficits of SoSh. 45 million and SoSh. 66 million in 1973 and 1974 respectively.[44] As the foreign exchange reserves were depleted, import restrictions were introduced and consequently an acute shortage of goods in the domestic market occurred. The ensuing inflation considerably overvalued the SoSh. and paved the way for the emergence and thriving of the parallel market. Soon, traders started to smuggle SoSh. banknotes abroad. They sold the notes to Somali workers in the Gulf and used the proceeds for the importation of badly needed commodities into the country. The initial reaction of the authorities was harsh. Controls at ports and airports were tightened, and punishment for foreign exchange law offences was raised.[45] However, the gap between the official and parallel rates grew so large that the Somali workers were reluctant to use the official banking channels, and the prospect for profit was so attractive that the traders were willing to operate in the parallel market despite the risks involved.

To ease the acute shortage of goods in the market, the government introduced in 1976 a scheme known as "Franco Valuta."[46] Under this scheme, an importer who obtained foreign exchange abroad (from migrant workers) was automatically given permission to import goods into the country. This, in effect, amounted to a government recognition and legalization of the parallel market (the hitherto illegal black market, Table 1). Gradually, the scheme increased its scope both in terms of participants and transactions, and developed into a sizeable parallel market that overwhelmed the official one. For example, from 1986, exporters were allowed to retain 60 percent of their foreign exchange earnings and sell them at the parallel market. Later, the scheme was extended to landlords

---

[44] In the early 1970s, a joke was made to dramatize the incompetence of state enterprises. At that time, the government was fighting to no avail the sand dunes that spread to large tracts of agricultural land. This is the joke: Do you want the sand dunes to disappear quickly? Transfer their management to "E.N.C." The latter stands for Ente Nazionale per il Commercio or National Agency for Trade.

[45] Law No. 54 of January 1, 1975.

[46] Somali Democratic Republic, Ministry of Trade Circular, Mogadishu, 1976. Franco Valuta means own foreign exchange.

who leased houses to expatriates and foreign diplomats. In addition, the parallel market was regularly supplied with foreign exchange obtained from official channels at a lower exchange rate. Under the parallel market, the exchange rate depreciated continuously in response to market conditions and set the pace for the perennial devaluation of the Somali shilling.

Table 1. Exchange Rate Movements: 1971-1980 (Somali shillings per U.S. dollar)

End of period	Official rate	Parallel rate
1971	6.91	---
1972	6.91	---
1973	6.29	---
1974	6.29	---
1975	6.29	---
1976	6.29	7.00
1977	6.29	7.50
1978	6.29	8.50
1979	6.29	10.00
1980	6.29	14.00

Source: Central bank of Somalia and Interviews with moneychangers

The Crisis of the Somali Shilling 1980-1990

In June 1981, the Somali authorities adopted a stabilization program within a framework of a standby arrangement with the IMF. The objectives of the program were to close the growing gap between the official and the parallel exchange rates, attract foreign exchange resources into official channels, and curb the mounting inflationary pressure. Under this program, the Franco Valuta system was abolished, restrictions on foreign trade were eased, and a dual exchange rate system was introduced. Under the dual exchange rate system, the official exchange rate applied to some essential imports, and 100 percent devalued rate (SoSh. 12.5 per dollar) applied to all other foreign transactions. With that devaluation, the government embarked on a course of continuous and large devaluations chasing the parallel exchange rate (see Table 2). The sequence has been as follows:

- In 1982, the official rate was devalued to So.Sh.15.01 per U.S. dollar, while the parallel rate stood at SoSh. 24 per U.S. dollar.
- In September 1983, a managed floating system was introduced, under which the official rate devalued to SoSh. 17.0 per U.S. dollar, compared to a parallel rate of SoSh. 45.0 per U.S. dollar.
- In September 1984, the official rate was again devalued to SoSh. 26 per U.S. dollar against a parallel rate of SoSh. 87.0 per U.S. dollar.
- In 1985, the official rate was devalued several times to SoSh. 42.5 per U.S. dollar, while the parallel rate fell to SoSh. 115.0 per U.S. dollar.
- In 1986, the official rate was devalued by SoSh. 4 per month until it reached SoSh. 86.5 per U.S. dollar in October 1986.
- In September 1986, a system of foreign exchange auction was introduced. Under that system, foreign exchange was auctioned to successful bidders on a regular fortnightly basis, who used it for the importation of commodities into the country. The aim of the foreign exchange auction was to unify the different exchange rates and provide a stable and realistic exchange rate. However, under the auction system, the official rate depreciated from SoSh. 94.1 in November 1986 to SoSh. 159.9 per U.S. dollar in September 1988. Over the same period, the parallel rate, which was supposed to disappear, depreciated from SoSh. 120.0 to SoSh. 180.0 per U.S. dollar.
- Unhappy about developments in the exchange rate, the Somali authorities suspended the auction system in September 1987 and pegged the exchange rate at an unrealistic rate of SoSh. 100 per U.S. dollar. That rate soon proved ineffective and consequently the auction system was reintroduced.[47]
- In June 1988, a managed floating system was reintroduced, and the official rate was devalued to SoSh. 180 per U.S. dollar. Thereafter, the exchange rate was adjusted on a weekly basis. By December 1990,

---

[47] Abdirahman Jama Barre was appointed as Minister of Finance. He criticized the devaluation of the Somali Shilling and arbitrarily set the exchange rate at SoSh 100.00 per dollar. His intention was, as he declared, to make the shilling a strong currency. Apparently, he did not fully grasp the forces behind the depreciation of the shilling, of which the most important one was excessive government expenditure. Likewise, many government leaders did not see the link between government deficits and the depreciation of the Somali shilling. As explained by the Theory of Currency Crisis (Krugman 1979), devaluation is the result of a fundamental inconsistency between domestic policies – uncontrollable issue of money to finance persistent budget deficits – and the attempt to maintain a fixed exchange rate.

the official rate stood at SoSh. 4,500 per U.S. dollar compared to a parallel rate of SoSh. 5,500 per U.S. dollar.

Table 2. Exchange Rate Movements: 1981-1990 (Somali shillings per U.S. dollar)

End of period	Official rate	Parallel rate
1981	6.295*	20.00
1982	15.206	24.00
1983	17.556	45.00
1984	26.000	87.00
1985	42.500	115.00
1986	90.500	140.00
1987	100.000	250.00
1988	270.000	460.70
1989	930.000	1742.00
1990	4500.000	5000.00

Source: Central Bank of Somalia and interview with moneychangers.
*From June 1981, there was a second exchange rate of SoSh. 12.59 per U.S. dollar.

As is evident from the foregoing, the adjustment program failed to close the gap between the official and the parallel exchange rates as well as stabilize the shilling; and the reason was that the government's monetary and fiscal policies were out of control.[48]

---

[48] Important figures about the money supply were concealed from the IMF. However, the one figure the government could not conceal was the black market exchange rate. And on the basis of that indicator, the IMF ordered massive devaluations of the Somali shilling, which fueled the inflationary pressure, and eroded the real income of the population, especially the poor.

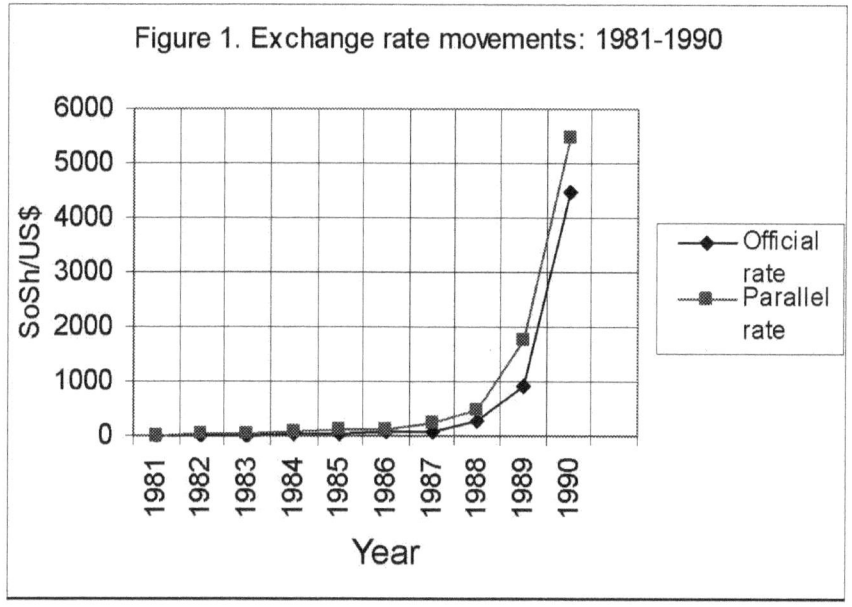

Figure 1. Exchange rate movements: 1981-1990

Exchange Rate Developments 1991-2001

The Market

With the collapse of the Somali State, many national institutions faded away, but not the foreign exchange market. On the contrary, it grew bigger, more vibrant, and more competitive than in the past. Several factors explain this development.

First, the market benefited from the absence of government controls, restrictions, and harassment. Although the parallel market was tolerated by the government in the late 1980s, it did not, however, enjoy official sanction. As a matter of fact, dealers in the market were often harassed by the police, and in general operated in a legally uncertain environment. This is not the case now.

Second, the remarkable increase in the inflow of remittances from the Somali diaspora, estimated at U.S. $750 million to U.S. $1 billion per year,[49] provided the market with a sizeable and reliable source of foreign exchange, which gave rise to an extensive and an elaborate remittances transfer system. To be more accurate, the money transfer system or Hawala is not new and, in fact, predated the Civil War. As noted elsewhere in this

---

[49]   UNDP (2003).

book, during the Franco Valuta period (1976-1990), merchants used to travel abroad to mobilize remittances from Somali migrant workers and used the foreign exchange thus acquired to finance their import business. What is new, however, is the rise of myriad money transfer companies that specialize in remittance transfer, thus divorcing the money transfer business from that of import financing. Over the years, these companies have built the structure, the resources, and the expertise to transfer funds not only to Somalia but also to any part of the world instantly and at minimal rates of service fees. They have also started performing some banking functions such as the taking of non-interest-bearing deposits and the issuing of vouchers.

The money transfer companies operate in all parts of Somalia crossing clan lines, and have established a worldwide network of offices and agents. Competition among the money transfer companies has resulted in improved services and a significant reduction in service fee rates, which now range from 1 percent to 5 percent, depending upon the size of the remittance and the place of destination.

A typical Hawala transaction goes this way: An agent takes in the money from a Somali emigrant and notes in a register the amount, the full name and telephone number of the sender, as well as the full name and address of the recipient; the address being the clan and sub-clan particulars of the recipient or simply a telephone number. The remittance is then wired immediately to the company's headquarters (often in Dubai) by means of fax or e-mail, and from there to an agent in Somalia who arranges for the funds to be delivered to the recipient anywhere in Somalia, even in small, remote villages. At regular intervals, the agent transfers the collected funds to the company's accounts in Dubai or elsewhere using the traditional international banking channels. Often, transactions in opposite directions cancel out, but from time to time, remittances companies have to carry cash to Somalia under heavy security arrangements. The income from the remittances operations is shared between the agents and the owners of the company. Approximately 30 percent goes to agents, 45 percent covers the cost, and 25 percent is distributed to the shareholders as dividends.[50]

The U.S. dollar is used exclusively as the currency of transfer. This became necessary as different factions issued their own banknotes causing continued depreciation of the Somali shilling and introducing an element of confusion into the market.[51]

---

[50] Reported by Al-Barakat.
[51] Report for ILO Mission. "The Role of Remittances on Economy in Somalia."

Since the September 11 attacks, the Hawala system has been under international scrutiny and threat because of the suspicion that terrorists use the system to move money to their operatives around the world. In particular, one company, Al-Barakat, the largest money-transfer company in Somalia, was accused of being a money-mover for terrorists. Consequently, on November 7, 2001 the U.S. President, George W. Bush, froze the assets of Al-Barakat because of its alleged links with Osama bin Laden. Several days later, Al-Barakat's international telecommunications services were cut off, a move which forced the company to effectively shut down. However, Al-Barakat officials have persistently denied the allegations and stated their willingness to open their books to any interested authority. Before its closure, Al-Barakat used to handle U.S. $140 million of remittances a year (80 percent to Somalia), operated a network of offices and agencies in thirty countries, and reported an annual net profit of $700,000 from its money transfer operations alone.[52]

Following the closure of Al-Barakat, the United Nations felt obliged to intervene in order to avert a humanitarian disaster stemming from the closure of remittances companies which are a lifeline to millions of Somalis. Accordingly, in 2002, the UNDP launched, with the help of other donors, the Somali Remittance Project to "legitimize remittance services offered by the Somali money transfer companies and eventually bring them under internationally established banking rules and regulations.[53] As a result of the UNDP's efforts, a number of activities were undertaken, namely:

1. A UNDP Somalia team went to the U.S., UK, Norway, and the United Arab Emirates to meet with governments and financial institutions and to emphasize the importance of the remittance companies to the Somali economy;
2. A two-day workshop was held in Dubai for remittance companies and the Somali business community on the possible expansion of financial services in Somalia:
3. A two-day conference was held in London, which was attended by representatives of remittance companies, financial regulators from Britain, continental Europe, and the United States. The conference aimed at assisting remittance companies in developing a better understanding of the regulatory regimes that govern them; and financial sector regulators in gaining a better understanding of Somali

---

[52]   *Financial Times,* November 11, 2001.
[53]   UNDP, April 2002.

remittance companies and their efforts to formalize their operations.[54]

4. During the conference, fourteen remittance companies launched a new body, the Somali Financial Services Association, which aims to provide advocacy and technical support to the Somali remittance companies[55]; the fourteen remittance companies include: Towfiiq Nationlink, Amal Express, Kaah Express, Salaama Express, Dalasan Inter, Kalkaal, Hamdi Express, Sahan C. Broker, Mustaqbal Express, Olympic, Amana Express, Hilac Express, and Tawakal Express.

5. The Central Bank of United Arab Emirates completed the formal registration of all Somali remittance and clearing companies as part of UNDP's initiative to ensure that the flow of money to Somalia remains open.[56]

Lastly, an inexpensive and easily accessible telecommunication system greatly facilitated the speedy flow of remittances to Somalia. It also helped disseminate information about the exchange rate, making the market more transparent. Money transfer companies use an impressive array of telecommunication facilities, including the Internet, mobile telephone, fax, and HV radios to transfer funds from one place to another and from one customer to another at a record speed that is envied by international banks.

Exchange Rate Movements

As noted above, the exchange rate system of Somalia in the period 1991-2001 can rightly be described as a classic case of a floating exchange-rates regime; a regime in which the rate fluctuates freely in response to the interplay of market forces, or the interaction between the buyers and sellers of foreign exchange in the marketplace. For example, if the harvest is good, or more livestock is exported, or more remittances and international aid are received, the shilling appreciates. An opposite situation, of course, causes the shilling to depreciate, e.g. the ban on livestock or reduction in the level of remittances and foreign aid, or an increase in the demand of foodstuffs following a drought. But, the one factor that, by far, influenced the movement of the exchange rate of the Somali shilling is the introduction

---

[54] UNDP, December 2003.
[55] IRIN News, Nairobi, December 5, 2003.
[56] *Khaleej Times,* June 25, 2004.

of fake banknotes into the market. And this supports the arguments that the monetary approach to exchange rate determination applies to Somalia (see page 7). In other words, excessive monetary creation, before and after the Civil War, is responsible for the massive depreciation of the Somali shilling.

Information about exchange rates is dispersed quickly. In fact, a list of exchange rates is published daily in local newspapers and even posted in the Internet, and periodically broadcast over the BBC Somali Service. The U.S. dollar remains by far the dominant currency in the economy and serves as a unit of account and a means of payment for large transactions. Other widely used currencies include the Kenyan shilling, the Ethiopian birr, the Saudi riyal, and the UAE dirham.

The Somali foreign exchange market consists of the moneychangers who set the exchange rate based on the relative supply and demand for dollars and Somali shillings. Principal foreign exchange markets include Mogadishu's Bakaraha, Bossaso, and Hargeysa. Currency exchange rates may vary somewhat regionally depending upon the availability of U.S. dollars and shilling stocks in different areas. However, the rates converge eventually as arbitrage transactions occur among the different markets.

Table 3 and Figure 2 show exchange rate movements of the Somali shilling vis-à-vis the U.S. dollar. Before the outbreak of the Civil War in January 1991, the parallel exchange rate, which provides a better indicator of market conditions, stood at SoSh. 5,000 per dollar. Immediately after the war, the exchange rate plunged to SoSh 7,600 per dollar, reflecting the insecurity caused by the Civil War and the ensuing dramatic flight from domestic currency.[57] The rate remained extremely weak throughout 1991 mainly because of the huge injection of currency into the market by Ali Mahdi, the former Mogadishu North faction leader. Had it not been for this sizeable inflow of cash into the market, the exchange rate would have recovered to its pre-war level. In fact, by the end of 1992, as the notes brought in by Ali Mahdi had been exhausted, the rate appreciated remarkably by 40 percent, to SoSh. 4,200 per dollar.

In 1993, the shilling further strengthened to SoSh. 4,000 per dollar as the United Nations Office for Somalia (UNISOM) brought in and spent huge amounts of dollars in Somalia.

Between 1995 and 1998, the shilling remained weak but relatively stable, ranging between SoSh. 6,500 and SoSh. 8,000 per dollar. This was due to several factors: Faction leaders printed limited quantities of notes,

---

[57]   Michel Del Buono and Jamil Mubarak. *The Macroeconomy of Somalia, a conceptual view.* UNDOS. Nairobi 1999.

the cash was put in circulation in small amounts, and the economy needed some injection of liquidity due to the depletion of the old Somali shilling banknotes.

However, from 1999, the exchange rate of the Somali shilling experienced a dramatic trend of depreciation as private businessmen started importing successive and huge quantities of fake banknotes to earn the windfall seigniorage revenue. The exchange rate reacted wildly to each importation of currency or the rumor that such importation was forthcoming. For example, in April 1999, after businessmen imported a consignment of fake banknotes, the exchange rate jumped from SoSh. 8,500 to So.Sh. 10, 000 per dollar. Another consignment arrived in June 1999 and the exchange rate fell to SoSh. 11,000 per dollar. Yet another shipment came in October 2000, causing the exchange rate to drop to SoSh. 13,000 per dollar.

The importation of the counterfeit money accelerated after the inauguration of the Transitional National Government in October 2000, as the government depended on some traders for funding and, more importantly, as the hopes and expectations of the Arta Conference to produce a functioning government faded away. Unscrupulous traders, some of them allied to the government, started importing shipment after shipment of fake banknotes in November 2000, in February 2001, and in April 2001, driving the exchange rate to SoSh. 19,000 per dollar. By the end of 2001, the rate plummeted to an all-time low of SoSh. 24,000 per U.S. dollar.[58] The depreciation of exchange rate was also exacerbated by the continued ban on livestock exports to Saudi Arabia which was imposed in September 2000.

Since 2002, the Somali shilling has shown some remarkable stability, hovering around 19,000 to 20,000 per dollar. This stability has to do with the denomination of the currency which puts a limit to the amount of money that the warlords and faction leaders can print. As noted elsewhere in this book, when the government of Somalia collapsed, the highest currency denomination in existence was the 1,000 Somali shillings note (see the picture on page 22). Because of this fact, the importers of fake currency

---

[58] Interestingly enough, the importation of banknotes is more inflationary when carried out by the faction   leaders than when it is done by businessmen. The latter tend to be somehow restrained in injecting the cash into the market so as not to cause a sharp deterioration of the exchange rate as this cuts into their profit margin; whereas, function and government leaders tend to spend the money for political and military purposes and care less about its inflationary impact.

cannot print currency indefinitely. In fact, when the exchange reaches the level of SoSh. 22,000 per dollar, the printing and importation of fake currency are no longer profitable, as the cost of manufacturing exceeds the face value of the 1,000 Somali shilling note (see Box 4: Seigniorage on page 66). On the other hand, the importers of fake currency cannot introduce new currency with higher denominations, to increase their profit margin, because these will not be accepted by the public as Ali Mahdi notes experienced. This is fortunate, as it prevents the warlords from creating inflation indefinitely.

Table 3: Exchange rate movements 1991-2001 (+) depreciation
(-) appreciation

End of period	SoSh./ U.S. $	% Change
1991	7,000	+27.3
1992	4,200	-40.0
1993	4,000	-4.7
1994	5,000	+25.0
1995	6,500	+30.0
1996	7,500	+15.4
1997	8,000	+6.0
1998	8,300	+3.5
1999	10,000	+21.2
2000	13,000	+30.0
2001	22,500	+73.1

Source: FAO/GIEWS Special Reports on Somalia, local newspapers, BBC Somali Service, UNDOS, Internet sources.

The Somaliland Shilling

The Somaliland shilling (SLSh.) was introduced in October 1994 at the rate of SLSh. 50

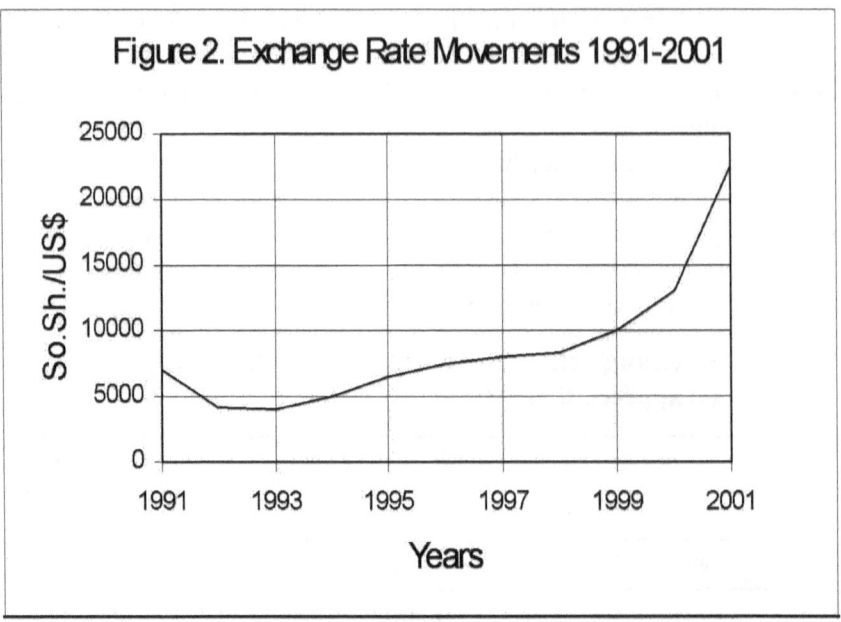

Figure 2. Exchange Rate Movements 1991-2001

per 1 U.S. dollar. Soon after its introduction, the SLSh. started losing ground and suffered as badly as the Somali shilling. By December 1995, the Somaliland shilling exchanged at SLSh 332 per U.S. dollar, registering a huge depreciation of 564 percent. The depreciation was triggered by the importation of large quantities of banknotes by the Somaliland administration. Further quantities of notes were imported in 1996 and, as a result, the rate plunged dramatically to SLSh. 5,400 per 1 U.S. dollar (see Table 4 and Figure 3). So severe was the depreciation that merchants refused the Somaliland shilling and demanded payments in U.S. dollars in defiance of the government's attempt to impose the use of the official exchange rate and the introduction of price controls. However, from 1997, the SLSh. strengthened substantially as the government stopped printing currency, and introduced some measures of financial discipline. By December 1999, the SLSh. appreciated to SLSh. 2,850 per dollar. From 2000, the SLSh. started depreciating mainly because of the ban on livestock exports and poor financial discipline.

As far as currency management is concerned, the authorities in Somaliland have shown that they are no better than the faction leaders who irresponsibly print fake currency. Witness the dramatic fall of the Somaliland shilling from SLSh. 50 per dollar in 1994 to SLSh. 7,000 in December 2001. In the opinion of one observer:

"The government's [Somaliland] attempts to support the national financial system failed. An example: the government tried to support Somaliland-shilling by sanctioning foreign exchange operations and by fixing the exchange rate, which caused strong public protest. Many traders threatened the government with moving their activities to Puntland in Eastern Somalia, where there are no restrictions for export trade. Even though the parliament dropped this unpopular decree in 1996, the economy is still very suspicious to state policy. Economic mainactors blame the government for extreme inflation in 1996 as well. For the state tried to compensate enormous budgetary deficit by printing money."[59]

The use of the Somaliland shilling is not only limited geographically (it circulates in western and parts of eastern Somaliland), but also in terms of economic agents. "In Somaliland, because of de facto dollarisation, the local currency is only effectively used by low-income households—nomads, farmers, petty traders and civil servants."[60]

The Somaliland shilling resembles the old Somali shilling of the 1980s in many ways. It has a dual exchange rate, the official exchange rate set by the government and the free market rate determined by the market. It is printed in large amounts to cover the large government deficit, which leads to sharp and continuous depreciations, a big and ever- growing gap between the two rates, and loss of confidence in the Somaliland shilling. To tackle this problem, the government resorts to price and exchange control measures. As these measures fail to stabilize the currency, the government blames the moneychangers and the so-called currency speculators for the monetary chaos. For example, *The Jamhuuriya* newspaper of 4th October 2000 published a circular (one of many of its kind) issued by the governor of the Somaliland Central Bank in which he warns "against the hoarding of Somaliland notes with a view to causing inflation and the depreciation of the Somaliland shilling"; and "calls upon all those concerned to stop causing economic crisis and work towards returning the foreign exchange rates to where they were a few months ago." He further warns that, "if such regulations are violated, the government will take stern measures and, if necessary legal actions, to return the economy to the right path." The right path means the artificial official exchange rate.[61]

---

[59]   "Politics and Economy in Nation-building Processes: Somaliland Republic." Paper presented by Tabea Zierau (University of Hanover), VAD 2002.

[60]   *Dr. Ismail Ibrahim Ahmed,* "Borrowing From the Poor: The Cost of Uncontrolled Money Printing in Somaliland." *The Somaliland Times.* July 5, 2004.

[61]   Source: Somalilandnet.com.

Table 4. Exchange rate movements: Somaliland shilling 1994-2001

December	SLSh/U.S. dollar Free market rate	% Change (-) appreciation
1994	50	
1995	332	564
1996	5,400	1,526
1997	3,500	- 35
1998	3,900	11
1999	2,850	- 27
2000	5,140	80
2001	7,000	36

Source: Somaliland, Ministry of National Planning and Coordination. BBC Somali Service.

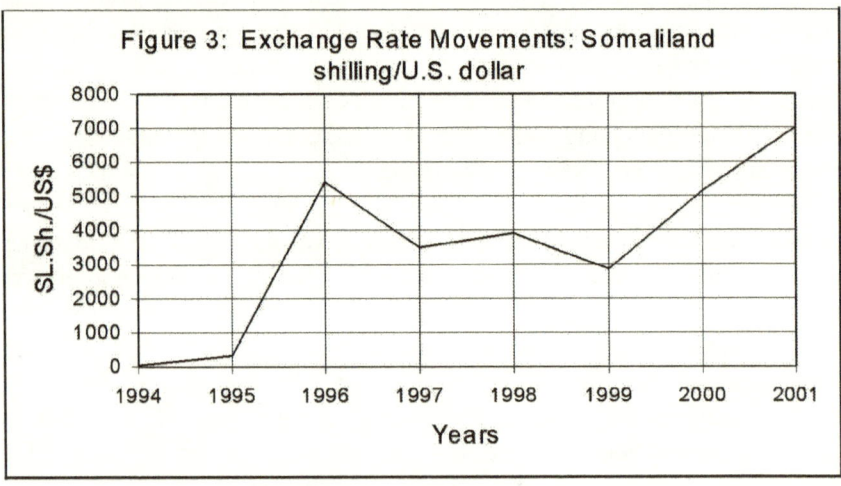

Figure 3: Exchange Rate Movements: Somaliland shilling/U.S. dollar

---

[61] Source: Somalilandnet.com.

IV
MONEY SUPPLY, EXCHANGE RATES AND INFLATION

The sharp and continuous depreciation of the Somali shilling that we have seen in the previous chapter was due to the high volume of liquidity injected into the economy through expansive monetary and fiscal policies. Excessive monetary creation fueled the inflationary pressure, which in turn led to further depreciation, plunging the economy into a vicious circle of inflation-depreciation-inflation.

In this chapter, we will review monetary developments during the period 1961-2001, examine the causes behind the excessive monetary expansion, and discuss the link between money supply, exchange rates, and inflation. To begin with, the relevant variables will be defined as follows:

- Money supply is defined as the stock of total monetary assets (broad money). These comprise currency in circulation, demand deposits, and savings deposits. These are, in fact, the only monetary instruments that were available in Somalia. It is worth noting here the composition of demand deposits, which consist of current accounts (checking accounts) and circular cheques "jeegagga wareega." The latter are banker's drafts that were widely used in Somalia in place of personal cheques. Originally, the circular cheques were intended for small payments and transfers, but, over time, they became a widespread and convenient means of payments and replaced cash for settlement of big transactions. As will be discussed below, circular cheques had proven to be an uncontrollable source of monetary creation by the Commercial and Savings Bank of Somalia (CSBS).

- Money supply data have to be examined with caution. This is so because the banks, especially CSBS, experienced some difficulties in reporting data accurately and on timely basis. Poor communication between the headquarters and the branches coupled with inadequate and dubious accounting practices caused considerable delays in reporting data (not excluding elements of book-cooking and data manipulation).[62] Nevertheless, the figures reveal the trend experienced in those years.

- Exchange rate is the nominal rate that measures the relative price of the Somali shilling in terms of the U.S. dollar. The official rate is the one published by the Central Bank of Somalia (CBS), while information on the parallel rate is supplied by private dealers.

- Inflation rate is measured by the consumer price index of Mogadishu, which is based on a Mogadishu family budget survey in 1985. It used to be published by the Ministry of Planning.

- Information on printed fake currency was obtained from different sources, including UN reports, Internet sources, local and international newspapers, and interviews with traders and former bank officials.

Money Supply 1961-1970

Table 5. Money supply 1961-1970 (in billions of SoSh)

	Dec. 1961	Dec. 1970	**% change**
Money in circulation	0.08	0.15	**88**
Demand Deposits	0.08	0.23	**188**
Savings Deposits	0.02	0.09	**350**
Total	**0.18**	**0.47**	**161**

Source: *International Financial Statistics Year Book,* IMF, Washington, 1991

---

[62] The IMF program contained, as usual, some specific performance criteria that the government was required to meet. Unable to meet IMF targets, the government resorted to an elaborate strategy of data manipulation and concealment. At one time, the difference between the figures supplied to the IMF and the actual ones amounted to about SoSh. 6 billion.

Growth in money supply was relatively moderate during the period 1961-1970 as compared to the following periods of 1971-1980 and 1981-1989 (see Table 5.) It expanded from SoSh. 180 million at the end of 1961 to SoSh. 470 million at the end of 1970, or 161 percent. Over the same period, currency in circulation nearly doubled to SoSh. 150 million. Demand deposits expanded by SoSh. 150 million or 188 percent while savings deposits increased strongly by SoSh. 70 million or 350 percent.

Table 6. Domestic credit 1961-1970 (in billions of SoSh)

	Dec. 1961	Dec. 1970	% change
Credit to Government	--	0.06	
Credit to Public Entities	--	0.04	
Credit to Private Sector	0.04	0.30	**650**
Total Domestic Credit	**0.04**	**0.40**	900

Source: *International Financial Statistics Year Book,* IMF, Washington, 1991

What causes money supply to expand? Generally, monetary expansion can come from two sources: increase in domestic credit (credit to the private sector and credit to the government and public enterprises) and increase in net foreign reserves (inflow of net foreign exchange). Since the increase in net foreign reserves is usually minimal due to endemic balance of payments problems, domestic credit remains as the most important determinant of monetary growth in the case of Somalia. This means that credit developments explain, to a large extent, the behavior of the exchange rate and the inflation rate and, therefore, need to be analyzed in more detail.

Table 6 shows credit aggregates for the period 1961-1970. At the end of 1961, total domestic credit outstanding amounted to SoSh. 40 million, entirely owed by the private sector. By the end of 1970, total domestic credit reached the figure of SoSh. 400 million, of which over 72 percent represented credits to the private sector. Claims on central government stood at SoSh.60 million. The government's position was little changed from 1966 as the government's credit ceiling was regularly observed in those years. The government had a borrowing limit of 35 percent of the average actual revenues of the last three years. When that limit was reached, credit to the government was curtailed, a feat which could not be repeated in later periods. Credit to public enterprises stood at SoSh. 40 million in December 1970. The entire amount was recorded in the year

1970 as the new socialist government started establishing new public enterprises.

Money Supply 1971-1980

Table 7 and Figure 4 display money supply statistics for the period 1971-1980. As can be noted, money supply grew sharply from SoSh. 0.39 billion in December 1971 to SoSh. 3.38 billion in December 1980, or 766 percent compared to a growth of 161 percent recorded during the preceding period of 1961-1970. The sharpest increase was recorded by currency in circulation, which expanded from SoSh. 0.15 billion in December 1971 to SoSh 1.51 billion in December 1980 or 906 percent. Demand deposits and savings deposits grew by 605 percent and 900 percent respectively.

Table 7. Money supply 1971-1980 (in billions of SoSh)

	Dec. 1971	Dec. 1980	% change
Money in Circulation	0.15	1.51	**906**
Demand Deposits	0.18	1.27	**605**
Savings Deposits	0.06	0.60	**900**
Total	**0.39**	**3.38**	766

Source: *International Financial Statistics Year Book,* IMF, Washington, 1994.

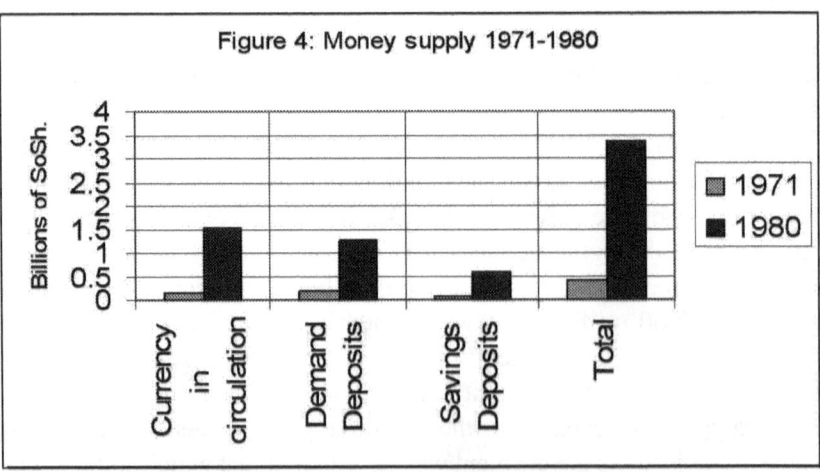

Figure 4: Money supply 1971-1980

Let us examine the sources of money supply expansion during this period. As shown in Table 8 and Figure 5, total domestic credit increased from 0.33 billion in December 1971 to SoSh. 3.88 billion in December 1980. The bulk of the increase in credits went to the government (SoSh. 1.87 billion) and to the public enterprises (SoSh. 1.51 billion). Credits to private sector accounted for only 6 percent of the increase. The 1970s, as will be recalled, were the years when the government adopted Scientific Socialism and embarked on heavy-handed statist interventions in the economy, which swelled the public sector operations and its insatiable demand for credits.

Two important developments which accelerated the increase in public sector credits are worth mentioning here. First, as a result of the 1977 war between Somalia and Ethiopia, the government incurred huge expenditures, which were financed by the Central Bank through printing money. Second, the Franco Valuta system, introduced in 1976, was another factor that influenced the growth in domestic credits. Under this system, public enterprises purchased merchandise from the Franco Valuta importers at inflated prices and borrowed heavily from the banking system to pay for these purchases.

Table 8. Domestic credit 1971-1980 (in billions of SoSh.)

	Dec. 1971	Dec. 1980	% change
Credit to Government	0.03	1.90	**6,233**
Credit to Public Entities	0.04	1.55	**3,775**
Credit to Private Sector	0.25	0.43	**72**
Total	**0.33**	**3.88**	**1,075**

Source: *International Financial Statistics Year Book,* IMF, Washington, 1994

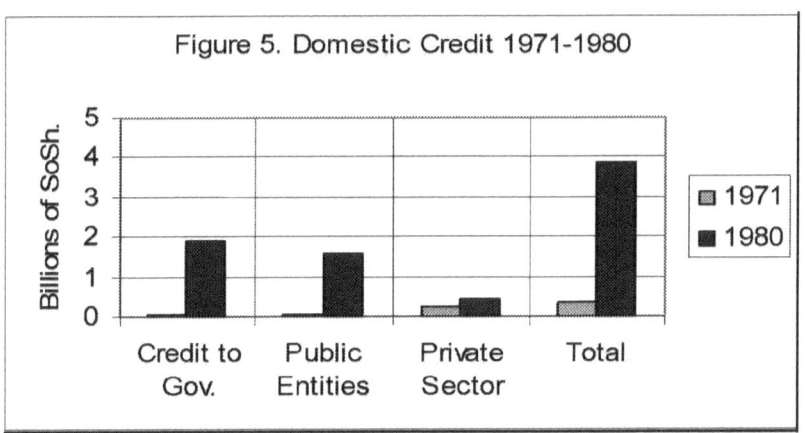

Figure 5. Domestic Credit 1971-1980

Money Supply 1981-1989

During the period 1981-1989, money supply increased phenomenally from SoSh. 4.4 billion at the end of 1981 to SoSh. 157.99 billion at the end of 1989, which represents a spectacular growth of 3,474 percent (see Table 9).

Among the components of money supply, demand deposits showed the highest increase (3,778 percent) reflecting the massive volume of circular cheques issued by the Commercial Bank, which will be discussed later. Currency in circulation grew with an equally remarkable rate of 3,645 percent. Savings deposits went up by 2,321 percent.

It is worth noting that in just one year, 1989, money supply increased by a staggering amount of So.Sh. 97.9 billion. However, a word of caution is in order here. It is highly probable that part of these figures may belong to previous years. This could happen because of poor and dubious accounting practices. Still, these are huge numbers for one year, even discounting for the faulty accounting practices. When one considers that this explosive trend continued also in 1990, for which data are not available, one understands how far things got out of hand.

It may be interesting to see monetary developments in Ethiopia, a country that had suffered from civil war, famine, and influx of refugees as Somalia did. Figures show a sharp contrast with Somalia. In fact, during the period 1981-89 money supply in Ethiopia increased by only 148 percent compared to 3,474 percent recorded in Somalia (see above).[63]

Table 9. Money supply 1981-1989 (in billions of SoSh.)

	1981	1989	% change
Currency in Circulation	1.89	70.79	3,645
Demand Deposits	1.78	69.04	3,778
Savings Deposits	0.75	18.16	2,321
Total	4.42	157.99	3,474

Source: *International Financial Statistics Year Book,* IMF, Washington, 1994

---

[63] *International Financial Statistics Yearbook.* 1992, IMF, Washington, D.C.

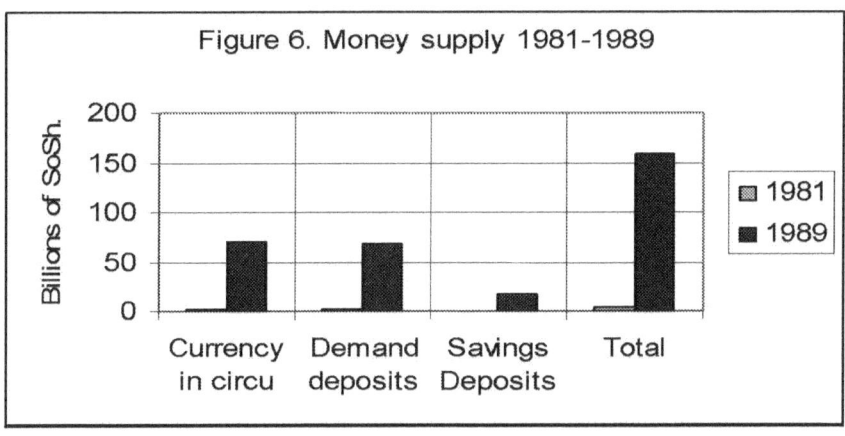

As was the case in the preceding periods, domestic credit was also the major factor that drove the expansion in money supply during the period 1981-1989. As can be observed from Table 10, total credits rose sharply by SoSh. 94.3 billion or 2,074 percent between December 1981 and December 1989. Credits to the private jumped from SoSh. 0.57 billion in December 1981 to SoSh. 89.79 billion in December 1989 and accounted for 90.7 percent of the increase in total credits (see Table 10). This is a complete reversal to the trend observed during 1971-1980, when credits to the public sector accounted for 94 percent of the increase in total credits. While in the 1970s, excessive monetary creation was driven by easy and bad credits to the public sector, in the 1980s, it was driven by easy and bad credits to the private sector. Consider this: Just in 1989, credits to the private sector rose by an enormous amount of SoSh. 60.15 billion, and most probably by a bigger one in 1990.

Table 10:   Domestic credit 1981-1989 (in millions of SoSh.)

	1981	1989	% change
Credit to Government	2.25	14.07	525
Credit to Public Entities	1.72	- 4.93	-187
Credit to Private Sector	0.57	89.79	15,653
Total	4.55	98.93	2,074

Source: *International Financial Statistics Year Book,* IMF, Washington, 1992

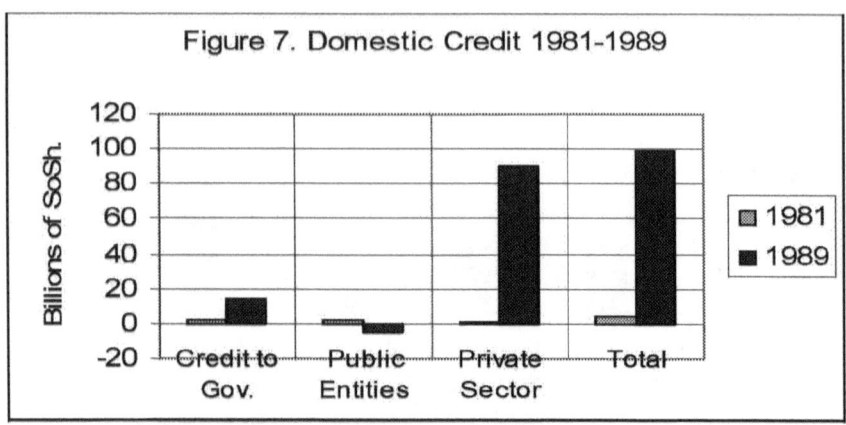

It is useful to examine the level of net foreign assets (reserves), which is an important factor that affects changes in money supply. An increase in foreign reserves causes money supply to expand, and a decrease makes it contract. Table 11 indicates net foreign assets during the period 1981-1989. As can be seen, net foreign assets decreased dramatically from a credit balance of SoSh. 60 million to a debit balance of SoSh. 214.3 billion.[64]

Table 11. Net foreign assets 1981-1989 (in billions of Somali shillings)

End of period	Foreign assets (net)
1981	0.06
1989	- 214.31

Source: *International Financial Statistics Year Book,* IMF, Washington, 1992

This means that net foreign assets had a contractionary effect on money supply. In fact, the increase in foreign liabilities reflected an inflow of foreign exchange through external loans. These loans were intended to mop up excess liquidity from the system and, therefore, help stabilize the exchange rate of the Somali shilling. An example was the auction scheme under which millions of U.S. dollars were sold in order to drain millions of Somali shillings out of the market and keep the money supply under control. This was not effective, however, because the banks, especially the CSBS, created more money than was absorbed by the foreign exchange

---

[64]   Total external debt of Somalia amounted to U.S. $2,034.7 million by the end of 1988. Source: IMF.

auction. To take an example, the last auction program, which ran from 1987 to 1990, sold around 30 million U.S. dollars. If we assume an average exchange rate of SoSh. 500 per dollar, which is very conservative, at least 15 billion Somali Shillings should have been withdrawn from circulation and the result would have been a strong Somali shilling.[65] This was not, however, the case. It is believed that many participants in the auction program were acquiring U.S. dollars with circular cheques obtained from the CSBS by means of generous and "ill-gotten" loans; some of them did not even import any merchandise into the country, but siphoned off the funds into private foreign accounts of their own.

In addition to credits, there were also two other factors that fueled the increase in money supply. These were uncontrolled and wasteful expenditures by the banks and government's misuse of the proceeds from the sale of commodities received as aid. In fact, both the treasury and the banks went into an incredible spending spree. They spent huge sums on construction, furniture, luxury cars, foreign trips, and on a wide range of other goods and services that should not have been bought except for corruption; looting might have been the right term.[66]

The Banking Crisis

In the early 1980s, credit to the government was the major factor behind the excessive monetary expansion. The war with Ethiopia, the influx of large numbers of refugees, natural calamities, and government profligacy necessitated huge expenditures that were financed through recourse to Central Bank borrowing. Later, however, the government position improved as a result of inflow of sizeable official grants and loans.

Unfortunately, while the government position was somehow improving, credits to the private sector grew out of control and stood as the major factor contributing to the monetary expansion. This happened because the CSBS, the only commercial bank at that time, became more politicized, successfully resisted Central Bank supervision, and indulged in widespread abuses, irregularities, and corruption. The Central Bank itself did not provide an example of financial discipline and integrity. It

---

[65] There were also other auctions selling food and agricultural inputs and equipment. The auction funds were channeled through the Italian Bank: Istituto Bancario San Paolo di Torino, which processed the letters of credit.

[66] To cite one example of a wasteful expenditure, the Central Bank built an auto repair workshop that did not become operational, for 10 million U.S. dollars out of the borrowed funds from the IMF.

also succumbed to corruption and political pressure, and became too busy rationing scarce foreign exchange resources.[67]

In a sound banking system, a commercial bank must keep a reserve of legal tender to meet any possible demand by its customers. This the CSBS did not do. Not only did the CSBS lend out all of its reserves, but also it issued uncovered circular cheques in large quantities and amounts. The situation became so critical that in mid-1989 the bank was literally unable to meet the demand of its depositors even for small amounts of cash. As if that were not enough, the bank continued to issue more circular cheques against new unsecured credits at a massive scale. This further aggravated the situation, and caused the worst banking crisis in the history of the country. The bulk of the circular cheques were cashed at high discount (20-40 percent) by private traders who used them for the payment of taxes and/or the purchase of foreign exchange in the auction system. In turn, this contributed to the depletion of reserves from the Central Bank, which was receiving only circular cheques, and led to an acute shortage of banknotes in the country with devastating consequences.[68]

Ironically, the authorities blamed the currency crisis on the public who allegedly hoarded cash as a plot to undermine the government's credibility. In fact, the president warned in a broadcast speech that those hoarding cash were doing so at their own risk, as the government could not guarantee their security. Also, the Central Bank was unjustly criticized for having failed to print enough currency, in the face of the massive increase in money supply during the last several years.

Under pressure, the Central Bank printed large quantities of banknotes and supplied a portion of them to CSBS on weekly basis, further swelling the volume of money supply. But, despite the continuous and substantial injection of liquidity, the fortunes of the CSBS could not, however, be reversed. For circular cheques were still being issued by corrupt and politically protected Commercial Bank branch managers, while the ability of the Central Bank to print more cash was constrained by lack of foreign exchange resources. To compound the problem, the president refused

---

[67]　For example, in a typical day the director general of the Central Bank spent most of his time either signing, promising, refusing, or delaying to sign the "D form," or the permit to purchase foreign exchange at the official rate. If one got the permit, he or she could profit handsomely by purchasing foreign exchange at the lower official rate and selling it at the higher parallel rate.

[68]　Every body hoarded cash and disposed of the circular checks. Grasham's Law, which says that bad money drives good money out of circulation, was operating here.

to authorize the printing of higher denomination banknotes, arguing that these would facilitate the smuggling of currency out of the country. Because of hyperinflation, the cost of printing exceeded the face of value of almost all of the denominations. In fact, the Central Bank could not afford to print new currency at the fast rate at which the demand for cash was increasing. Inflation eroded the purchasing power of the shilling so much so that bundles of banknotes were required to make even small basic purchases; and hence the increased demand for cash. At one time, the Bank owed several million U.S. dollars to the banknote printing company, being unable to pay the bills on time.[69]

By early 1990, the situation was out of control and the CSBS totally lost the confidence of the public, and practically ceased to act as a financial intermediator. Its role was taken on by a multitude of small, private parallel banks that held abundant cash and discounted circular cheques at heavy discount rates. A group of Somali elders who wrote an open letter to President Siad Barre (the Manifesto Group) described the situation of the Commercial Bank in May 1990 as follows:

"All the doors of the Somali Commercial and Savings Bank had been practically closed to all clients for the past eight weeks as of today, and it is now commonly believed that the bank is totally bankrupt to the point of being thirty billion shillings in the red. This has come about as a result of political and tribal interference and pressure brought to bear on the managerial banking authority from the highest government circle, that ended up in facilitating easy credit to the tune of hundreds of millions of shillings, to the wives, the sons, the daughters, brothers and other relatives; as well as tribesmen and other political favorites of the governing echelon most of which later proved irrecoverable, since they were not covered or guaranteed by any assets or equities."[70]

In July 1990, the government adopted a comprehensive financial sector reform within the framework of an IMF sponsored program. The most important measures adopted in the program were the following:

    i)   A new commercial bank, the "Somali Commercial Bank," was established by the government, and started operations

---

[69] At the end, it was agreed to print 500- and 1,000-shilling notes. While the Central Bank could not afford to print currency because of the costs involved, the Commercial Bank did not face such financial constraints in issuing circular cheques. The latter were printed cheaply and locally and in large denominations, e.g. So.Sh. 500,000 and 100,000.

[70] Somali Elders Manifesto Memo to General Mohamed Siad Barre. 15 May 1990.

in August 1990. The initial capital of the bank was SoSh. 1 billion, paid up by the Ministry of Finance (50 percent) and Central Bank of Somalia (50 percent). Private businesses were allowed in principle to buy shares into the new bank and take over the ownership and management of the bank within a year. The objective of establishing a new bank was to fill the gap left by the CSBS and, in general, to introduce some competition in the banking business.

ii) The CSBS was instructed to stop any new issues of circular cheques.

iii) The CBS was instructed to cease granting any further loans and advances to the CSBS.

iv) Circular cheques were declared no longer valid for the payment of taxes and/or purchase of foreign exchange in the auction system.

v) It was decided that the Central Bank pay in cash up to 20 percent of all deposits owed by the CSBS to its customers within August 1990. The remaining balance of deposits will be paid by the CSBS through loan recovery.

By the time the negotiations of financial sector reform were completed, the situation was out of control politically, economically, and militarily. The rebel movements, which were fighting the government since the early 1980s, were closing in on Mogadishu, the capital, while inflation, by wiping out the value of wages, turned government soldiers, who were supposed to defend the regime, into street vendors (see Appendix B).

Money Supply: 1991-2001

Following the outbreak of the Civil War, the banking system vanished as other state institutions. In fact, the banks were looted, their buildings vandalized, and their records destroyed. In particular, the doors of the Central Bank were blown apart, its safes were blasted, and all cash and other valuables were looted. Stale lower denomination banknotes littered the streets outside the Central Bank for days (see the pictures on page 58).

Table 12 and Figure 8 show currency issued between 1991 and 2001. As can be seen, a massive amount of currency (SoSh. 595 billion) was issued during that period. The bulk of this money was created in the last three years, when businessmen and faction leaders competed to print and distribute as much cash as they could.

Table 12. Currency Issued: 1991-2001 (in billions of Somali shillings)

Year	Currency issued
1991	80.0
1992	24.0
1996	32.5
1999	118.0
2000	130.5
2001	210.0
Total	595.0

Source: Internet sources, local newspapers, UNDOS, and United Nations' reports, National Post.

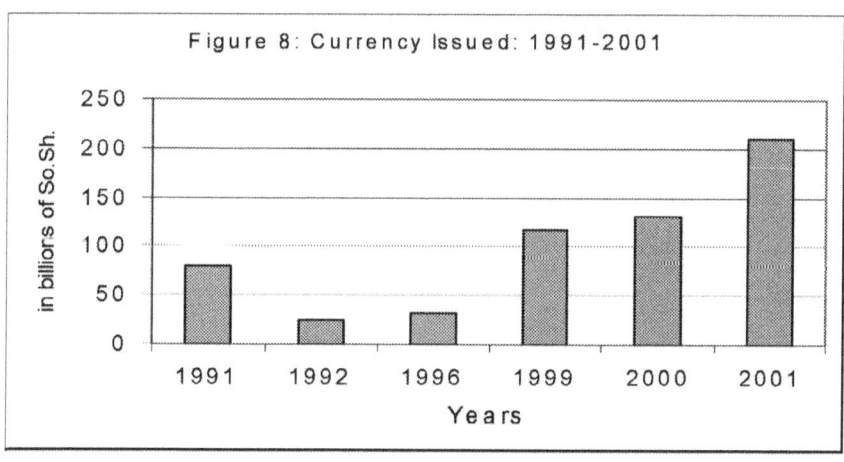

Figure 8: Currency Issued: 1991-2001

Devastated Central Bank building

Devastated Commercial Bank building

Table 13 shows the parties that issued currency during the period under review. Hussein Aideed and businessmen of his kin led the way by issuing the largest portion of banknotes worth SoSh. 165 billion. The money, printed in Canada, arrived in Somalia in several batches and destabilized the fragile economy. The first batch, worth about SoSh. 35 billion, arrived in Mogadishu in late 1966 just after the death of General Mohamed Farah Aideed, and was received by his son, Hussein Aideed.[71] The second batch, worth SoSh. 35 billion, was imported by businessmen of Aideed's clan, as Hussein lacked enough financial resources to meet the cost of the printing. He attempted to block the operation, but the dispute was settled after a sum of money was allocated to him (about SoSh. 2.5 billion).[72] The same businessmen imported the balance, worth about SoSh. 90 billion, in three successive batches in 1999 and 2000.[73]

In 1991, Ali Mahdi received SoSh. 80 billion worth of banknotes ordered and paid for by the former government of General Mohamed Siad Barre before its collapse in December 1990. He also received in 1992 another consignment of banknotes worth SoSh. 24 billion, of the type known as "N" currency. That money was also ordered by the former Somali government and was intended to replace the old Somali shilling.[74]

Businessmen associated with the Transitional Government imported SoSh. 90 billion. The notes were imported in three planeloads in February 2001 by Mohamed Deylaf, a prominent businessman and a financier of the Transitional Government.[75] The interim government was obliged to buy a portion of the money to mitigate its inflationary impact, after being sharply criticized for allowing the importation of the fake currency into the country.[76] Another TNG financier who took part in the importation of the fake currency is Hussein Goley.[77] Also, the UN panel of experts reports that Khadija Ossoble Ali, a former TNG Minister of State, allegedly

---

[71]   *The Ottawa Sun* 29/10/2000. Hussein Aideed acknowledged that his faction ordered SoSh. 150 billion from a company in Canada. Source: Interview with Mohamed Xaji Ingriis, 16/02/2001.

[72]   *Xinhua,* April 9, 1999.

[73]   *The Ottawa Sun* 29/10/2000.

[74]   UNDOS, November 1999.

[75]   The notes arrived at Ballidogle Airport, 90 km south of Mogadishu, and were driven to Mogadishu in fifty armed vehicles and guarded by 600 militia. Source: *Qaran Newsletter,* February 12, 2000.

[76]   *Xog-Ogaal,* 12 February 2001. The TNG has also sold 1 million U.S. dollars in Mogadishu's main Bakaraha market, with funds obtained from Saudi Arabia, in an attempt to raise the value of the shilling against the dollar.

[77]   Maxamad xaaji (Ingriis). Hiiraan Online February 12, 2001.

ordered a consignment of counterfeit currency from Indonesia on behalf of the TNG in 2002.[78]

Puntland and businessmen from the same region brought in SoSh. 86 billion. The notes were printed in Indonesia by Peter Pura Baru Kudus Factory under the authorization of Colonel Abdullahi Yusuf, the then president of Puntland, with Mr. Ahmed Mohamed Goala, the former head of Puntland Bank, negotiating the contract.[79] Part of this money (around SoSh. 10-15 billion) was delivered to Colonel Hassan Mohamed Nur (Shatigadud), chairman of Rahanweyn Resistance Army (RRA), in Baidoa, in May 2000.[80]

Table 13. Currency issued by issuer 1991-2001 (in billions of Somali shillings)

Issuing Party	Currency Issued
Ali Mahdi (includes SoSh. 24 billion 'N' currency)	104.0
North Mogadishu businessmen ('N' currency)	90.0
Aideed & businessmen	165.0
Transitional Government & businessmen	90.0
Puntland & businessmen	86.0
Independent businessmen	60.0
Total	595.0

Source: Internet sources, local newspapers, UNDOS, and United Nations' reports.

---

[78] Report of the Panel of Experts on Somalia Pursuant to the Security Council resolution 1474 (2003).

[79] Report of the Panel of Experts on Somalia.

[80] As reported by Ayaamaha 20 May 2000, the delivery was made possible by a tripartite agreement between Colonel Abdullahi Yusuf, Colonel Hassan Mohamed Nur and Eng. Munye, a businessman who profits from operating fishing vessels owned by the previous Somali government.

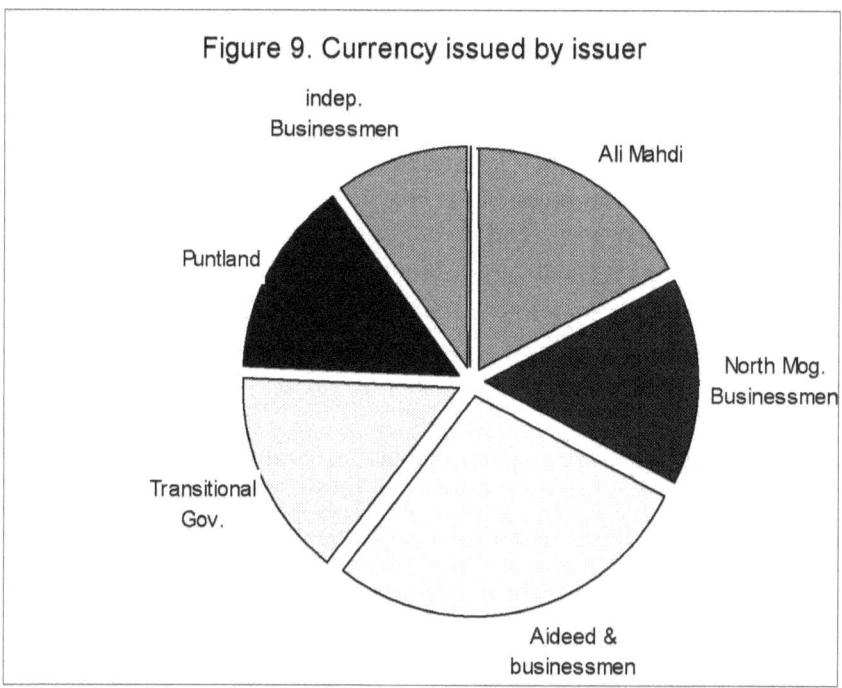

Figure 9. Currency issued by issuer

About SoSh. 60 billion worth of banknotes were imported by businessmen not affiliated to any particular faction.

Traders from North Mogadishu imported SoSh. 90 billion of the type "N" currency. The notes, which were reportedly printed in Malaysia, arrived in Isiley Airport, thirty kilometers north of Mogadishu in July 2000.[81] The printing of "N" currency is very economical as one "N" shilling is worth a hundred old shillings, but its circulation is limited to North Mogadishu and adjacent areas.

Accurate data on money supply in Somaliland are not available; nor do the Somaliland authorities disclose how much money is printed and how much is put into circulation. According to some reports, in 1994 and 1996, the Somaliland authorities issued banknotes worth more than SLSh. 19 billion, a fact which caused the Somaliland shilling to plunge. Information about later issues is not available, but thought to be substantial.[82]

In the previous section, we have seen that credits were the major factor responsible for the excessive growth of money supply during the period 1971-1989. In a way, we can say that the quantity of printed fake money represents also a credit given to the warlords and their associated

---

81 *Xog-Ogaal,* August 1, 2001.
82 UNDOS, Nairobi 1999.

businessmen as they obtain goods and services in exchange for new pieces of paper, or rather a hidden tax exerted by them on the poor population; and these are the nomadic pastoralists, the poor dependent on wage labor, street vendors, and petty traders. In this sense, there is no difference between when the previous government issued money and now that a faction leader or a businessman prints it. In each case, the notes were used for political purposes, and in each case, the result has been the same: hyperinflation and economic devastation.

The Link Between Money Supply, Exchange Rates, and Inflation

Having discussed developments in monetary aggregates and identified the major cause behind the excessive monetary expansion, we will now examine the link between money supply, exchange rates, and inflation rates.

1961-1970: This period was remarkable for its stability. The annual inflation rate was, on average, 3.4 percent, money supply grew at an annual average rate of 13.4 percent, the shilling was strong, there was no black market of any significance, foreign trade was free, and the financial system was sound. This stability was achieved through the implementation of stabilization measures limiting the growth in domestic credit (Table 14).

Table 14. Money supply, parallel exchange rates, and inflation rates 1961-1980 (average % change)

	Money Supply	Parallel Exchange Rates	Consumer Price Index
1961-1970	13.4	---	3.4
1971-1980	63.8	9.4	6.9

Source: *International Financial Statistics Year Book,* IMF, Washington, 1991

1971-1980: The seeds of the runaway inflation and currency crisis experienced in the 1980s were sown in this period. To carry out its nationalization policies, the government established some forty or so public enterprises, with no adequate capital, no qualified personnel, and no sound accounting and management systems. Furthermore, it ordered the banks to extend unlimited credit facilities to the newly established enterprises. This lax credit policy created inflationary pressure that was masked by price and exchange controls. Repressed inflation manifested itself in long queues, commodity shortages, black markets, and rationing.

1981-1989: Table 15 and Figure 10 show movements in money supply, parallel exchange rates, and inflation rates during the period 1985-1989.[83] Generally, the figures reveal a noticeable relationship between the three variables. Over the period under review, on average, money supply increased by 92 percent, parallel exchange rates by 99 percent, and inflation by 59 percent. However, one can distinguish between two periods. In the first period of 1985 to 1987, money supply increased faster than the depreciation in exchange rates and the rise in prices. This is explained by the inflow of grants and loans in favor of the government, which partly absorbed monetary expansion and therefore offset its inflationary impact. In the second period, 1987-1989, the exchange rate depreciated more rapidly than the growth in money supply. It is in this last period that currency substitution (dollarization) has emerged, as people became more sensitive to exchange rate depreciation and the rapid loss of purchasing power. As a result, any new addition to the money supply triggered a bigger amount of depreciation.

Table 15. Money supply, parallel exchange rates and inflation rates 1985-1989 (changes in percent)

	Money Supply	Parallel Exchange Rates	Consumer Price Index
1985	81.1	32.2	37.6
1986	34.0	21.7	35.8
1987	127.1	78.5	28.1
1988	57.2	84.3	81.7
1989	162.8	278.1	110.4

Source: *International Financial Statistics Year Book,* IMF, Washington, 1991, and private traders.

---

[83]   The 1985 base was chosen because a new Consumer Price Index was established in that year.

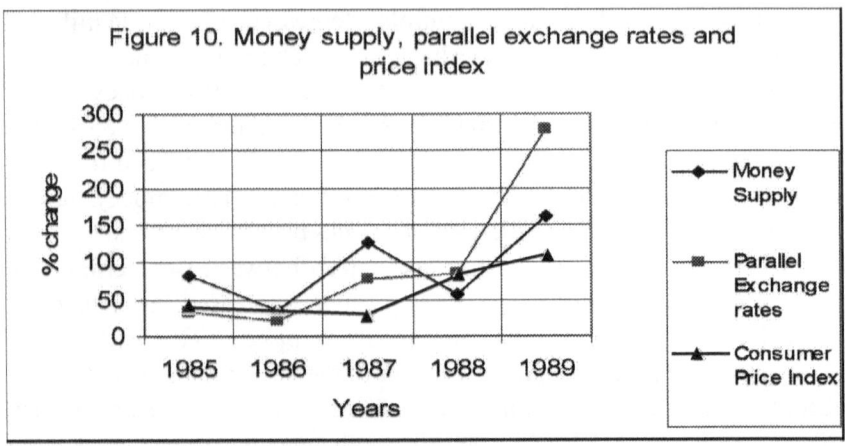

Figure 10. Money supply, parallel exchange rates and price index

1991-2001: There are no accurate and systematically collected and published statistics on money supply and consumer price index in the period 1991-2001 due to the absence of a national government and a national monetary authority. However, the available data shows a clear relationship between money supply and exchange rate movements, especially in the last three years, when more information was available. Despite the absence of a consumer price index, it is a well-known fact that prices rose sharply every time a consignment of fake banknotes arrived in the country. Sometimes the prices rose above the depreciation rate. The importation of fake currency and the inflation it caused were widely reported by newswires, local and international newspapers, UN reports, BBC News, and by a host of other observers. The galloping inflation affected ordinary people's everyday lives by eroding the value of their meager incomes and hampered the smooth flow of the business activities as wholesale traders refused to accept the Somali shilling.

The 2001 Human Development Report for Somalia notes: "The most dramatic influence on the cost of living in the past three years has been the currency crisis that has triggered hyperinflation and eroded the purchasing power of poorer households."[84] A clear indicator of the existence of hyperinflation is the fact that the 500-shilling banknote has become worthless and unacceptable as medium of exchange.[85]

Also, the Food Security Assessment Unit, which monitors food security situations in Somalia, reported in May 2001:

---

[84]   UNDP Somalia (2000) *Human Development Report.* Page 72.
[85]   "Mustaqbalka 500 Sh.so oo mugdi ku jira." BBC Laanta Somaaliga, 03-10-2001. London

"The inflation rate is at its highest point since the early 90s. Markets and consumers are experiencing extreme financial instability as newly printed Somali shillings continue to enter the market. Combined with the livestock ban, the following groups are badly affected: small traders, livestock traders, casual labourers, Internally Displaced Persons and government employees; poor pastoralists are also experiencing hardship"[86]

The importation of fake currency attracted the anger and the indignation of the public, and triggered street riots and protests in Mogadishu, Bossaso, and Burao. In Mogadishu, two people were killed by market guards after a crowd rioted following the importation of a new consignment of banknotes.[87] Religious scholars, business associations, social groups, and civil societies have condemned the importation of fake currency. In Mogadishu, thousands of Somali school children began a three-day strike in April 2001 to protest against the crippling economic effects of fake currency.[88] In Bossaso, people gathered at the football stadium to pray for rain and against the fake currency.[89]

---

[86] FSAU/FAO, *Monthly Food Security Report for Somalia,* May 2001.

[87] BBC News, June 28, 1999.

[88] IRIN 18th April 2001.

[89] "Somalia's Monopoly money." *Cairo Times.* May 2001.

Box 4. Seigniorage

In all countries, currency issue is a state prerogative. Not so in Somalia, where banknotes are imported for profit like any ordinary merchandise. Since 1991, about 595 billion Somali shilling notes have been imported by an assortment of businessmen, warlords, function leaders, and regional administrations, and these generated huge profits (seigniorage) to the issuing parties. What is seigniorage? To explain what seigniorage is, let us go back a bit into history. Originally, only gold and silver coins were used as money. The coins had an intrinsic value; that is, their face value was equal to their purchasing power or the value of the metal contained in them. As the feudal lords who minted the coins needed more funds, they started debasing the money by putting less silver and gold into the coins, and thereby making a profit from the difference between the face value of the coins and their cost of manufacturing. That profit is called seigniorage after *seigneur* (lord) in French. With the introduction of banknotes, which are cheaper to print, the gap between the face value and the cost of manufacturing (seigniorage) has increased substantially.

According to some Somali businessmen, it costs U.S. $0.028 to manufacture a note of 1,000 Somali shillings, the highest denomination banknote. Initially, the importers of fake currency reaped a windfall seigniorage profit equal to 250 percent of the face value of the notes. That was when the exchange rate stood at SoSh. 10,000 per dollar. However, as more notes were printed, more inflation ensued, causing more depreciation and less seigniorage revenue. For example, at the current exchange rate of SoSh. 22,000 per dollar, the seigniorage profit falls to 50 percent and shrinks further when transportation, storage, and security cost are taken into account. Thus, the fact that the highest denomination is 1,000 shillings means that the importers of fake currency cannot create inflation indefinitely. And that explains why the Somali shilling is still in circulation. Lately, some businessmen started printing the "N" currency, which is more profitable as one "N" shilling is equal to one hundred old shillings. But the circulation of "N" currency is limited to north Mogadishu and adjacent areas.

Seigniorage revenue entails some heavy social costs or suffering. For one thing, it is an oppressive hidden tax (inflation tax) extracted mainly from the poor, the rural population, and the small-scale traders who have no access to foreign exchange resources. For another, it bankrolls the militias and thus prolongs the destructive civil war in the country.

V

A CURRENCY BOARD SYSTEM
FOR SOMALIA

As pointed out in the introduction, during the 1980s and 1990s, the Somali shilling had suffered from massive depreciations, which, in turn, caused financial chaos, currency collapse, and economic ruin, and largely contributed to the fall of the Somali government and the perpetuation of the endless cycle of violence in the country. Excessive and reckless printing of currency for personal and political gains has been the root cause of this financial crisis.

To stop the financial chaos and restore monetary stability, I recommend the introduction of the Currency Board system in Somalia. Stability is essential for economic development. It allows people to plan their business decisions with confidence; it facilitates trade, enhances investment, and provides an environment conducive to economic growth. Stability is also important for social considerations. Usually, it is the poor who suffer most from the ravages of devaluation and inflation. In fact "The people most affected by the swings in the currency market are those who do not hold reserves of foreign currency, the rural population, the poor dependent on wage labor, street vendors and petty traders, who make the bulk of population."[90]

Generally, there are two ways to conduct monetary policy in pursuit of economic and financial stability. One way is to focus on the exchange

---

[90] UNDP Somalia (2001) *Human Development Report,* Nairobi. Page 113.

rate and fix it against the currency of a country with strong monetary policy credentials and thus benefit from this policy in terms of low inflation and stable exchange rate. The other way is to use the interest rate or money supply to put the inflation rate under control. This option, however, may not be available to Somalia, as there is no money market, no banking system, and no market-determined interest rate of any kind in Somalia. This leaves the fixed exchange rate as the only monetary policy option open to Somalia. The reasons why the fixed exchange rate system is appropriate for Somalia are discussed in chapter three in more detail (see page 18).

The currency board system is preferred because it is the most credible fixed exchange rate arrangement. Also, it is simple, transparent, and relatively easy to implement. Most importantly, it provides an effective way "to stop currency chaos, limit corruption, and establish stability."[91]

A number of countries successfully adopted the currency board system at a time of currency crisis. Hong Kong introduced its currency board in 1983 and still supports it enthusiastically. Lithuania, Estonia, Bulgaria, Bosnia & Herzegovina have fixed their exchange rates by means of currency board mechanism or variations thereof. Djibouti has been operating a currency board since 1949 through which it insured the stability of the Djibouti franc. Historically, Somalia has had a positive experience with the currency board system, as it belonged to the former East African Currency Board area. Argentina's currency board, however, collapsed in December 2001 after ten years of operation. Powerful external economic shocks, combined with poor fiscal discipline, made the currency board unsustainable over time. But, as *The Economist* puts it, although Argentina's currency board broke down, it is "wrong to declare currency boards a menace under all circumstances. For many countries— especially if they are small, open to trade and lacking a central bank with inflation-fighting credibility—they may be the best insurance against hyperinflation."[92]

There are also other strong arguments in favor of establishing a currency board system in Somalia at the present time. The currency board reinforces the free market economy now thriving in every part of Somalia as it guarantees the convertibility of the Somali shilling, which has been in effect for the last thirteen years.

---

[91] Steve H. Hanke, "How to Establish Monetary Stability," Testimony before the U.S. House of representatives, Committee on Banking and Financial Services, January 30, 1998.

[92] "Dollar Mad," *The Economist,* October 25, 2001.

Also, since the currency board is independent of political interventions, it removes a source of serious conflict. This is how conflict arises. Government leaders, or a few of them, enjoy uncontrolled power to print money. As a result, they are not interested in building up political consensus and in mobilizing domestic resources through taxation and self-help schemes. For their part, the citizens do not demand fiscal accountability since they are not paying taxes. Lack of accountability reinforces the prevailing culture of corruption and clanism and leads to a fierce competition over the distribution of easy money and eventually to civil war.[93]

The establishment of the currency board, however, requires strong leadership and commitment on the part of the government leaders as well as on the part of donor countries and agencies. This presupposes the end of the civil war, genuine efforts of reconciliation, and the formation of a representative and accountable central government.

If the currency board is not adopted, the alternative is de facto dollarization. Already the Somali economy is extensively dollarized, in the sense that, the dollar is now the predominant means of payment in Somalia. And the range of goods and services transacted in Somali shillings is rapidly shrinking as a result of the continuous importation of fake currency into the country. Actually, what prevents a full dollarization of the Somali economy is the unavailability of lower-denomination dollar coins. The widespread use and acceptance of the U.S. dollar by the public restricts the options available to the government. Either a sound and credible currency, one that is fully backed by foreign reserves, is provided, or else the U.S. dollar becomes legal tender in the country. For this reason, the currency board is recommended, because it brings the same benefits of dollarization, and in addition it earns substantial amount of seigniorage and offers a way to retain the national currency.

---

[93]   The war between two warlords, Mohamed Farah Aideed and Ali Mahdi, was in part caused by a quarrel over money. Aideed was angry that Ali Mahdi had privately imported "New Somali Shilling" banknotes to pay his militias. (*Reuters* 27 April '95 by Aden Ali).

Foreign aid is also a source of conflict, as it empowers the warlords. As *Bernhard Helander points out,* "Militia strength and the ability of factional leaders to hijack Somalia's future is a function of the levels of influx of dollars and aid. The more funds that come in, the more likely it is that the artificial factions will be able to continue to cling on to aspirations for power." ("Somalia: aid fuels the conflict" .Bernard Helander, Uppsala University.)

Operating the Currency Board

As described in chapter two, a currency board is a monetary authority that issues notes and coins in exchange for a reserve currency at a specified fixed exchange rate. Unlike the Central bank, a currency board cannot print money at will, since it is required to maintain foreign reserves equal in value to the total amount of notes and coins in circulation. Thus, the core features of a currency board are the fixed exchange rate, the reserve or anchor currency, and full convertibility.

Anchor currency: The U.S. dollar should, logically, be the anchor currency as it is the most widely used and accepted currency in Somalia, in addition to being the dominant international currency.

Exchange rate: As to the exchange rate, the prevailing market rate at the time of the establishment of the board will be adopted, e.g. SoSh. 20,000 per dollar.

Reserves: At any given time the currency board should maintain dollar reserves equal to 100 percent of the value of the notes and coins in circulation. This will ensure the unlimited convertibility of the shilling into U.S. dollars.

Relation to government: By law the currency board is prohibited from lending money to the government or public enterprises. Even government deposits should not be held at the currency board in order to put the government at arms' length from the currency board. This means that the government should finance its budget with what it can raise through taxes, or proceeds from international aid, and not through recourse to printing money and thereby creating inflation.

By constraining the ability of the government to print money, the currency board disciplines the government and forces it to rethink about its priorities, and learn to live within its means. As the International Crisis Group points out, "economic realities in the country [Somalia] make clear that a future central authority will necessarily have extreme modest revenues. The sooner state-building goals reflect this, the better."[94] Or, as the UNDP report puts it more emphatically:

"Like a post-Cold War cargo cult, Somali political leaders continue to believe that if they can cobble together as an internationally-

---

[94]   "Somalia: Countering Terrorism in a Failed State," ICG, Africa Report No.45 page 28.

recognised state, funds will again flow into the coffers. Few have fully grasped the changed nature of international politics since the end of the Cold War and the failed intervention in Somalia. Few understand that, for the first time in its history, the Somali State will have to rely primarily on resources generated internally."[95]

Given this reality, one cannot justify a cabinet composed of eighty-six ministers and vice ministers, which has been the tradition in Somalia at the present.

Relation to banks: The currency board is prohibited from lending money to the banks. This means that the currency board has no responsibility to bail out insolvent banks. It follows that commercial banks must rely on other sources for lending of last resort. Generally, "a currency board would be much easier to operate if all banks were foreign, supervised by the monetary authorities of other countries, and with access to their lender-of-last-resort facilities."[96]

By cutting off credit to banks, the currency board disciplines also the financial institutions and forces them to adopt sound and prudent lending policies. As explained in chapter four, one of the factors that contributed to the financial crisis of 1980s was bad loans made by the commercial bank in the latter part of the 1980s. The bank was able to give away huge amounts of bad and dubious loans thanks to the availability of unlimited and automatic refinancing from the central bank. A UNDP report writes: "The financial sector, which was entirely owned by the public, was largely a financing tool for public agencies that often were working for either the army or the security or the closest clients of the regime."[97]

By providing a stable currency, the Currency Board will play the role of a catalyst for the development of a well-functioning financial sector comprised of commercial banks, development banks, savings banks, cooperative banks, credit unions, and finance companies. Joint ventures between Somali private banks and foreign banks should be encouraged.

As for the supervision and regulation of the banks, a department within the Ministry of Finance can do the job, or an office specially established for that purpose.

Outstanding currency: The currency board cannot redeem the fake banknotes currently in circulation unless dollar reserves of equal value

---

[95]   UNDP. Somalia 1999 Human Development Report. Nairobi.

[96]   Stanley Fisher, Central Banking: The Challenges Ahead, Maintaining Price Stability, Finance and Development, Vol.33 # 4, December 1996.

[97]   UNDP Somalia (1998) Human Development Report. Nairobi.

are provided, which is unlikely. One option is to let these notes circulate alongside the currency board notes until they wear out over time.

Management: The currency board will be governed by a board of directors representing the shareholders. To protect the currency board form political pressure, representatives from international financial or aid organizations, and Somali businesspersons should be represented in the board and even hold the majority of the shares so as to exercise effective control over the currency board.

Profit: The currency board realizes profit from the difference between the interest earned from the assets held in U.S. dollars and its operating costs. A part of these profits could be allocated as reserves and the rest paid to the shareholders in proportion to their contributions.

Advantages of Currency Board

The biggest advantage of the currency board system is the depoliticization of the process of money creation. By prohibiting the financing of government budgetary deficits, the currency board system prevents corrupt governments from printing money at will. This is extremely important in the case of Somalia, as the involvement of politicians was behind the financial chaos that inflicted so much damage on the economy and on the people.

The currency board also guarantees an automatic balance of payments adjustment. For example, a deficit in the balance of payments creates an outflow of foreign exchange and reduction in domestic money supply. The fall in money supply brings about a decline in prices and a contraction in income, which will lead to a reduction in imports and ultimately the elimination of the balance of payments deficit. The opposite occurs in case of a surplus (Box 5).

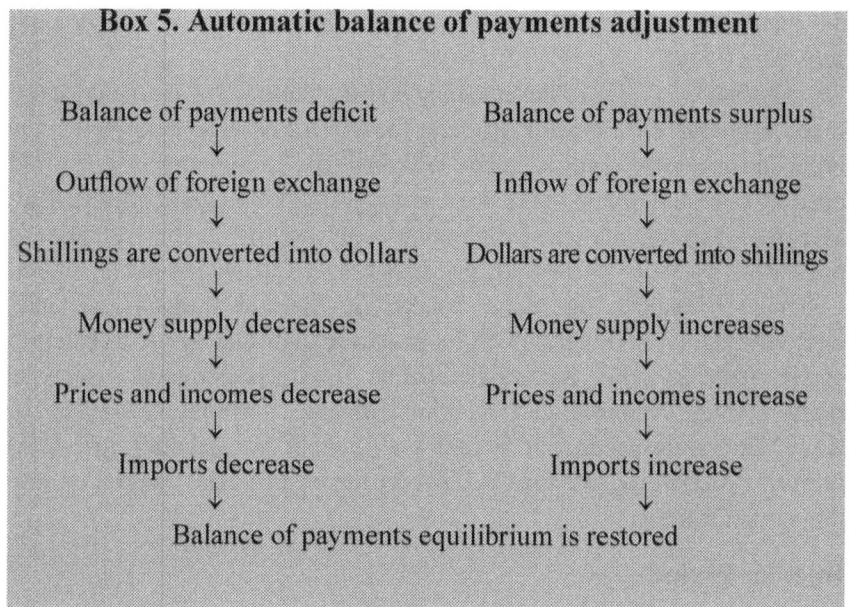

Box 5. Automatic balance of payments adjustment

Balance of payments deficit
↓
Outflow of foreign exchange
↓
Shillings are converted into dollars
↓
Money supply decreases
↓
Prices and incomes decrease
↓
Imports decrease
↓

Balance of payments surplus
↓
Inflow of foreign exchange
↓
Dollars are converted into shillings
↓
Money supply increases
↓
Prices and incomes increase
↓
Imports increase
↓

Balance of payments equilibrium is restored

Other strong benefits of the currency board system are price stability, stable exchange rate, and currency convertibility, which result from the imposition of strict fiscal discipline. The resulting stable economic environment promotes trade, investment, and economic growth.

Yet another advantage of the currency board is its simplicity. It needs a small number of staff. It is also transparent, in the sense that a breach of the currency board's rules will be obvious to all.

Disadvantages of Currency Board System

A currency board system is criticized for being inflexible and not allowing the use of discretionary monetary policies to suit a country's own economic conditions. In fact, the monetary base (notes and coins) is automatically determined by changes in the balance of payments. For example, a deficit in the balance of payments, and the resulting outflow of foreign reserves, causes the monetary base to contract, and hence the interest rate to rise sharply. However, this may not be the case in Somalia as the incidence of large speculative capital outflows or inflows are minimal and there is no market determined interest rate of any kind. A likely scenario would be a contraction in economic activities resulting from the balance of payments deficit, which if protracted could be a cause for concern. But the currency board, by creating a stable environment, will most likely attract direct investment, especially from Somalis in the Diaspora, which will more than offset any slowdown in economic activities.

Another weakness of the currency board system is that it precludes use of the exchange rate as an instrument for correcting balance of payments imbalances. As the local currency is linked to a strong currency, it could become overvalued and make the country's exports uncompetitive. But, as experience has shown, devaluations—by adding to the inflationary pressure—do more harm than good to a small economy like Somalia. Consider livestock, the main source of Somalia's export revenue. Understandably, devaluation will be powerless in affecting the production of livestock as other factors determine livestock population such as rainfall, range resource access, animal disease, and market conditions. It will be counterproductive in that it will cause skyrocketing prices for imported foodstuffs, and thus will hinder the pastoralists' integration into the market system.[98]

Interim Period

During the period when the cuurrency board system is being established—which may take some time—the U.S. dollar can be used as legal tender in Somalia. Already the Somali economy is widely dollarized. It is a matter of importing lower denomination dollar bills and coins and carrying all transaction in U.S. dollars at least as government business is concerned.

Conclusion
The currency system is preferred because of its simplicity, predictability, and rule-based nature. Furthermore, it provides a stable and convertible currency, promotes greater stability of domestic prices and the exchange rate, and as a result, enhances confidence. And confidence is of crucial importance, given the high rates of inflation and pervasive exchange rate instability experienced throughout the 1980s and 1990s, not to mention the public's mistrust of government leaders and the feuding of different regional clan-based factions.

It should, however, be noted that the currency board system is not a panacea. Certainly, it cannot provide a magic solution to the country's economic problems, nor can it operate in an environment where other important supporting institutions are missing. And the mere introduction of a currency board does not necessarily guarantee fiscal discipline, for there

---

[98] FSAU, Focus, "Pastoralists under pressure," October 2001.

is a possibility that government leaders squander public funds collected as taxes or received as aid from external donors, as often happens in Somalia. Ultimately, it requires political will and commitment to respect the rule of law, accept fiscal discipline, and ensure accountability in managing government finances.

APPENDIX A
SENIOR MANAGEMENT OF
THE CENTRAL BANK OF
SOMALIA 1960-1990

Presidents

Dr. Abdi Aden Mohamed	1960-1964
Sheikh Abdi Haji Abikar	1964-1968

Governors

Dr. Abdullahi Ahmed Addow	1968-1969
Dr. Abdurahman Nur Herzi	1970-1975
Dr. Omar Ahmed Omar	1975-1978
Mohamud Jama Ahmed	1978-1984
Dr. Omar Ahmed Omar	1985-1986
Mohamud Mohamed Nur	1987-1989
Dr. Omar Ahmed Omar	1989- Oct.1990
Ali Abdi Amalow	Nov.-Dec.1990

Deputy Governors

Osman Haji Yusuf	1988-1989
Mohamed Hussein Farid	Oct.-Dec.1990

Director Generals

Dr. Francesco Palamenghi-Crispi	1960-1967
Rag. Emilio Giannini	1967-1967
Dr. Giuseppe Morasca	1967-1969
Dr. Omar Ahmed Omar	1970-1975
Said Mohamed Ali (Shef)	1975-1978
Mohamed Mohamud Nur (Shod)	1978-1987
Said Mohamed Ali (Shef)	1980-1982
Bashir Isse Ali	1982-1987
Ahmed Mohamed (I-Say)	1987-1989
Sharif Abubakar Mohamed	1988-1989
Mohamed Dalmar Abdurahman	1989- 1990
Mohamed Husein Farid	Apr.-Oct.1990
Fadumo Mohamed Siad Barre	Oct.-Dec.1990

APPENDIX B
THE CIVIL WAR: CHRONOLOGY OF EVENTS

In 1978, there was an attempted coup; the organizers escaped to Ethiopia and formed the first rebel movement, the Somali Salvation Democratic Front (SSDF). In 1981, the Somali National Movement (SNM) was formed, followed by the United Somali Congress (USC) in 1988. Later on, more rebel movements were formed along clan bases and put pressure on Siad Barre's regime.

In early 1990, a group of 114 prominent Somalis, known as "Manifesto Group" wrote an open letter to Siad Barre calling for his resignation.

On January 27, 1991, Siad Barre was ousted from power and forced to flee from the capital. Earlier, he tried to manipulate the clan system distributing modern weapons to clan militias. But the weapons were turned against him. The ousting of Siad Barre was followed by a cycle of lawlessness, abuse, violence, and reprisals by the USC militia against civilians.

On January 29, 1991, Ali Mahdi Mohamed was named interim president by USC, a move which angered other opposition movements.

On May 18, 1991, SNM proclaimed independence for Northern Somalia, formerly British Somaliland, and declared the formation of the "Somaliland Republic" but failed to receive recognition from the International Community.

In July 1991, peace talks aimed at ending Somali factional fighting took place in Djibouti. The "Djibouti Accord" was signed but soon became ineffective.

In November 1991, fighting intensified in Mogadishu between factions loyal to Ali Mahdi and General Mohamed Farah Aideed. The fighting caused 14,000 deaths and 27,000 wounded, according to Africa Watch estimates.

In April 1992, the UN approved sending military observers to monitor a cease-fire arranged by the UN in February 1992.

In May 1992, Siad Barre fled to Kenya after an ill-fated attempt to recapture Mogadishu. He later went to Nigeria to seek asylum.

In July 1992, UN Secretary General Boutros Boutros-Ghali alerts the world to the Somali disaster, observing that little attention was given to the "poor man's war." The UN estimated that 1.5 million Somalis were at that time in imminent danger of starvation.

On August 28, 1992, the UN Security Council calls for the dispatch of 3,000 soldiers along with 500 Pakistani soldiers destined for Mogadishu. After a number of delays caused by Aideed, the 500 Pakistani soldiers were stationed at Mogadishu Airport in November 1992. The Pakistani contingent was insufficient, ill-equipped, and remained stuck to their barracks at the airport.

Meanwhile, the Somali situation deteriorated into a human disaster of unprecedented proportions. An estimated 300,000 died as a result of drought, factional fighting, and looting of relief supplies by the warlords. Relief organizations estimated that as of September 1992, 25 percent of all Somali children under five years of age had died. Also, an estimated 1 million Somali refugees fled into neighboring countries.

In December 1992, the UN Security Council authorized the deployment of a multinational force by the United Sates in order to secure the distribution of food to the starving. The first U.S. soldiers in "Operation Restore Hope" landed in Mogadishu on the morning of December 9, 1993.

In March 1993, fifteen Somali factions met in Addis Ababa, Ethiopia in a reconciliation conference under the auspices of the UN. They agreed on a cease-fire, disarmament of the militias, and the establishment of a Provisional National Council. But these provisions were never implemented.

In May 1993, a force of 20,000 from twenty-seven nations took over the operation from the U.S.-led coalition.

In June 1993, twenty-four Pakistani soldiers were killed in an ambush. The UN accused Aideed of masterminding the ambush and issued a warrant to capture him and put him on trial. The incident sparked an urban guerilla battle between UN troops and Aideed supporters, which escalated into a heavy fighting on October 3, 1993, with nineteen UN soldiers dead, eighteen of them Americans. An American helicopter pilot was captured and later released. Somali casualties ran into the thousands.

On October 6, 1993, U.S. President Clinton announced that he was withdrawing the American troops by March 31, 1994. As planned, the U.S. forces completed their pullout from Somalia on March 26, 1994, leaving behind a UN force of 19,000 troops, which were withdrawn in March 1995.

On January 2, 1995, Mohamed Siad Barre died in Lagos, Nigeria reportedly of diabetes complications.

On August 1, 1996, Mohamed Farah Aideed died after being wounded in a Mogadishu battle between his forces on one part and those of Ali Mahdi, his archrival, and Osman Ato, his clansman and former financier, on the other. Aideed's son, Hussein, a former U.S. Marine, took command of his father's faction.

In January 1997, Somali factions announced, after six weeks of meeting in Sodere, Ethiopia, that they formed a Provisional National Salvation Council. They also pledged to form a national government in six months, but failed to carry through.

In December 1997, Somali factions met in Cairo, Egypt and signed the "Cairo Declaration" pledging to set up a national transitional government in two months, but again failed to implement their accord.

In June 1998, the UN political office for Somalia acknowledged the total failure of internationally and regionally sponsored peace agreements by Somali factions, and announced that it was launching a new "bottom-up approach." Under this approach, the UN will support leaders to form regional administrations and will concentrate on building institutions of civil society.

In July 1998, delegates from northeastern Somalia established, after seventy days of meeting in Garowe, a new regional state, the "Puntland State," but declared that they were not seceding from Somalia. They elected Col. Abdullahi Yusuf Ahmed as president. Some other regional factions declared their intention to establish their own regional states.

In May 2000, Somali delegates gathered in a conference in Arta, Djibouti, to embark on a peace process aimed at ending the civil war in Somalia.

In August 2000, a new Transitional National Government (TNG) was formed in Arta, Djibouti, which included a Transitional National Assembly as well as an interim president and prime minister. Abdiqasim Salad Hassan was elected as president. He appointed Ali Khalif Galayr as prime minister in October 2000. Some Somali groups and regional authorities remained outside the Arta peace process and denounced the formation of TNG.

In March 2001, seventeen faction leaders, opposing the Transitional National Government, met in Awasa, Ethiopia, and announced the formation of Somali Reconciliation and Reconstruction Council. They also announced their intention to form a national government in six months.

In June 2001, a controversy over Puntland's leadership started after Colonel Abdullahi Yusuf's mandate was extended by parliament for three years. A group of Traditional elders rejected the extended mandate and convened a general congress, which elected Jama Ali Jama as president of Puntland in November 2001. Meanwhile, Colonel Abdullahi Yusuf insisted that he remained the legitimate president of Puntland.

In November 2001, Ali Khalif Galayr lost a vote of no confidence in the Transitional National Assembly. Hassan Abshir Farah was appointed as his replacement.

In April 2002, a new regional administration, "the Somali Western State of Somalia," was announced in Baidoa. Hassan Mohamed Nur "Shatigadud" was nominated as the president of the South Western State of Somalia. However, the establishment of the South Western State led to a power struggle and severe fighting between forces loyal to "Shatigadud" and those of his two deputies Sheikh Adan Madobe and Mohamed Ibrahim Habsade.

In May 2002, Abdullahi Yusuf captured the port of Bossaso and ousted Jama Ali Jama.

In May 2002, Mohamed Ibrahim Egal, the president of Somaliland, died in South Africa after surgery. Somaliland's parliament inaugurated Vice President Dahir Riyale Kahin as president, in accordance with the terms of the Somaliland Constitution.

On October 15, 2002, Kenyan President Daniel Arab Moi opened the Somali National Reconciliation Conference in Eldoret, Kenya. The Conference, sponsored by IGAD, was initially attended by some 300 delegates, including 23 factional leaders, civil society representatives, and traditional elders. After twenty months of deliberations often marred by delays and disputes, a 275-member Transitional Federal Parliament was established on August 30, 2004. On September 15, 2004, Shariff Hassan Sheik Adan was elected as the new speaker of the parliament. On October 10, 2004, the new parliament elected Abdullahi Yusuf Ahmed as the president of Somalia for an interim period of five years. On November 4, 2004, President Abdullahi Yusuf, appointed Ali Mohamed Ghedi, a veterinarian and a former university lecturer as Somalia's new prime minister.

APPENDIX C
GLOSSARY

arbitrage: The process of buying a currency cheap in one market and selling it dear in another market.

auction: A method of determining price and interest.

balance of payments: A summary of the economic transactions between residents of one country and residents of other countries over a given period, usually a year.

balance of trade: That part of a nation's balance of payments dealing with imports and exports, that is trade in goods and services, over a given period.

bank note: A term used synonymously with paper money or currency issued by a bank. Notes are, in effect, a promise to pay the bearer on demand the amount stated on the face of the note.

bank supervision: Oversight of individual banks to ensure that they are operated prudently and in accordance with applicable statutes and regulations.

Bretton Woods: An international conference was held at Bretton Woods, New Hampshire, U.S.A., in July 1944, which led to the establishment of the International Monetary Fund and the International Bank for Reconstruction and Development (the World Bank).

capital account: One of two parts of a nation's balance of payments. The capital account is a record of all purchases of physical and financial assets between a nation and the rest of the world in a given period, usually one year.

capital market: A market for medium- to long-term financial instruments. Financial instruments traded in the capital market include shares, and bonds issued by governments, corporate borrowers, and financial institutions.

central bank: A non-commercial bank, which may or may not be independent of government, which has some or all of the following functions: conduct monetary policy; oversee the stability of the financial system; issue currency notes; act as banker to the government; supervise financial institutions; and regulate payments systems.

checking account: An account which allows the holder to write checks against deposited funds.

collateral: Property that is offered to secure a loan or other credit and that becomes subject to seizure on default.

contractionary fiscal policy: A policy to decrease governmental expenditures and/or to increase taxes.

contractionary monetary policy: A policy to restrict the growth of money and credit in the economy. See also **monetary policy.**

counterfeit: A representation of currency intended to deceive recipients.

currency: Notes and coins usually issued by the national government and used as medium exchange in a country.

currency appreciation: A relative increase in the value of one currency compared to another. The term is usually applied to a currency with a floating exchange rate system where the exchange rate is determined by market forces.

currency convertibility: A country's currency is convertible if any holder is free to convert it at market exchange rates into one of major international reserve currencies.

currency depreciation: A relative decrease in the value of one currency compared to another. The term is usually applied to a currency with a floating exchange rate system where the exchange rate is determined by market forces.

currency devaluation: A deliberate downward adjustment in the value of a country's currency relative to other currencies under a fixed exchange rate system.

currency revaluation: A deliberate upward adjustment in the value of a country's currency relative to other currencies under a fixed exchange rate system.

currency union: A group of countries that agree to share a common currency.

current account: One of two parts of a nation's balance of payments (the other is capital account). It is a record of all trade, exports and imports, services, and what's called unilateral transfers, between a nation and the rest of the world.

Current account: see **checking account.**

Default: Failure to meet the terms of a credit agreement.

deficit financing: Occurs when a government spends more money than it can raise by taxation or other means.

deflation: A sustained reduction in the general level of prices.

demand deposit: A deposit that may be withdrawn at any time without prior written notice to the depository institution. A checking account is the most common form of demand deposit.

denomination: The face value of a currency item: may be notes or coin.

dirty float: A type of floating exchange rate that is not completely freely floating because central banks intervene from time to time to alter the rate from its free-market level.

excess liquidity: The condition of countries' having too much money in circulation.

exchange control: Government regulations restricting or forbidding certain types of foreign currency transactions.

exchange rates: The price of local currency expressed in terms of another currency (or vice versa).

expansionary fiscal policy: A policy to increase governmental spending and/or a reduction in taxes. See also **fiscal policy.**

expansionary monetary policy: A policy of the Central Bank that is designed to expand the growth of money and credit in the economy.

fiat money: Money that has little or no intrinsic value as a commodity; it is costless to produce, usually taking the form of pieces of paper, and is not redeemable for any commodity.

financial institution: A company whose primary function is to intermediate between lenders and borrowers in the economy.

financial markets: A generic term for the markets in which financial instruments are traded.

financial sector: The sector of the economy that comprises financial institutions and financial markets.

fiscal policy: The government's decisions about the amount of money it spends and collects in taxes to achieve a full employment and non-inflationary economy.

fixed exchange rate system: Exchange rates between currencies are set at predetermined levels by the government and do not move in response to changes in supply and demand.

floating exchange rate: Exchange rates determined by market forces based on the demand for and supply of a currency.

foreign exchange: Money denominated in the currency of another nation or group of nations.

Franco Valuta: A system that permitted private traders to import goods into the country with foreign exchange obtained from migrant workers abroad.

hard currency: A currency widely accepted in foreign trade.

hard peg: Establishing a strong fixed exchange rate between one national currency (usually that of a small country) and another national currency (usually that of an industrial power).

IMF: An international organization of 183 member countries, established to promote international monetary cooperation, exchange stability, and orderly exchange arrangements; foster economic growth and high levels of employment; and provide temporary financial assistance to countries to help ease balance of payments adjustments.

inflation: A rise, over time, in the average level of prices.

lender of last resort: A country's Central Bank acts as "lender of last resort" by extending credit to the banking system in unusual circumstances involving a national or regional emergency, where failure to obtain credit would have a severe adverse impact on the economy.

liquidity: The capacity to sell an asset quickly without significantly affecting the price of that asset.

macroeconomics: The economy looked at as a whole or in terms of major components measured by aggregates such as gross domestic product, the balance of payments and related links, in the context of the national economy.

microeconomics: The study of economics in terms of individual areas of activity (as a firm, household, or prices).

money: Anything that is generally accepted in exchange as payment for goods and services. The emphasis is on "any," because any item or asset can serve as money, as long as it is generally accepted in payment throughout an economy.

money illusion: The confusion of changes in money values and changes in real values.

monetary policy: A Central Bank's actions to influence the availability and cost of money and credit, as a means of helping to promote national economic goals. Tools of monetary policy include open market operations, discount policy, and reserve requirements.

money supply: Total quantity of money available for transactions and investment.

official reserve assets: The Central Bank's holdings of foreign exchange, Special Drawing Rights, and gold.

overvalued currency: A currency whose exchange rate is below either its free market level or its long-term equilibrium level.

purchasing power parity theory: The exchange rate between any two currencies adjusts to reflect changes in the price levels within the two countries.

quantity theory of money: A theory that states a given percentage change in the money supply leads to an equal percentage change in nominal gross domestic product.

reserve currency: A convertible foreign currency which governments and international institutions are willing to hold because of its expected stability. The U.S. dollar is the major reserve currency in the world.

reserve country: The country that issues the reserve currency is called the reserve country.

seigniorage: The profit which results from the difference between the cost of making coins and currency and the exchange value of coin and currency in the market.

soft currency: A currency whose value is uncertain and which is therefore not widely accepted in foreign trade.

special drawing rights (SDR): A type of international money created by the International Monetary Fund (IMF) and allocated to its member nations. SDRs are an international reserve asset, although they are only accounting entries (not actual coin or paper, and not backed by precious metal). Subject to certain conditions of the IMF, a nation that has a balance of payments deficit can use SDRs to settle debts to another nation or to the IMF.

undervalued currency: A currency whose exchange rate is above either its free market level or its long-term equilibrium level.

REFERENCES

Africa Group of the Nordic Cooperation on Documentation. *Fact Finding Missions to Northeast and Northwest Somalia,* March, 1996.

Amnesty International. *Somalia: A Human Rights Disaster.* London, 1992.

Argy, Victor. *Exchange Rate Management in Theory and Practice.* Monograph series M66, Committee for Economic Development of Australia Study, February, 1982.

Austin, James E. *Managing in Developing Countries: Strategic Analysis and Operating Techniques.* New York: Collier Macmillan Publishers, 1990.

Bank for International Settlements. *Triennial Central Bank Survey of Foreign Exchange and Derivatives Market Activity.* Basle, 2001.

Bannock, Graham, R.E. Baxter, and Evan Davis. *Dictionary of Economics.* Sixth edition. Penguin Books, London. 1998.

BBC Laanta Soomaaliga (Somali Servicee). London.

Black, Stanley W. *Floating Exchange Rates and National Economic Policy.* New Haven: Yale University Press, 1977.

Bond, Marian E. *Exchange Rates, Inflation and Vicious Circles.* IMF Staff Papers vol. 27 No. 4 December, 1980. Washington D.C. IMF.

Boughton, James M. *The Monetary Approach to Exchange Rates: What Now Remains?* Essays in International Finance, International Finance Section, Princeton University, Princeton, NJ, 1988.

Central Bank of Somalia. *Annual Reports,* Various issues. Economic Research Department, Mogadishu.

Connally, Michael B, and Claudio Gonzalez-Vega (editors). *Economic Reform and Stabilization in Latin America*. New York: Praeger Publishers, 1987.

Destler, I. M. and C. Randall Henning. *Dollar Politics: Exchange Rate Policy Making in the United States*. Washington D.C.: Institute for International Economics, 1989.

de Waal, Dr. Alex. "Class and Power in Stateless Somalia." (Discussion paper). August 1996.

The Economist, "Getting out of a fix." September 20, 1997.

_____. "The Big Mac Index." April 25, 2002.

_____. "Dollar Mad?" October 25, 2001.

_____. "Spoilt for Choice." June 3, 2002.

_____. "No right answer." January 21, 2002.

Edwards, Sebastian and Ahamed Liaquat. *Economic Adjustment and Exchange Rates in Developing Countries*. Papers presented at Joint National Bureau of Economic Research - World Bank Conference, Washington D.C. 29 November - 1 December 1986. Chicago: The University of Chicago Press.

Edwards, Sebastian. "Exchange Rate Misalignment in Developing Countries," the World Bank occasional paper No. 2 new series. Washington, 1988.

_____. *Exchange rates, inflation and disinflation: Latin American Experience, in Capital Controls, Exchange Rates and Monetary Policy in World Economy*. Cambridge: Cambridge University Press, 1995.

_____. "The false promise of dollarisation." *Financial Times,* May 14, 2001.

Fisher, Stanley. "Central Banking: The Challenge Ahead, Maintaining Price Stability." Finance and Development, IMF/World Bank, Vol. 33 No. 4, December, 1996.

_____. "Exchange Rate Regimes: Is Bipolar View Correct?" Finance and Development IMF/World Bank, Volume 38, Number 2, June, 2001.

Food Security Analysis Unit. *Focus: Pastoralists Under Pressure*. Nairobi. October, 2001.

Gosh, Atis R., Anne-Marie Gulde, and Holger C. Wolf. "Currency Boards: The Ultimate Fix?" IMF Working Paper, International Monetary Fund, Washington D.C., 1998.

Gulhati, Ravi, Bose Swadesh, and Atukorala Vimal. "Exchange Rate Policies in Eastern and Southern Africa, 1965 – 1983." World Bank Staff Working Papers No. 720, Washington D.C., 1985.

Hanke, Steve H. "How to Establish Monetary Stability in Asia." Testimony before the U.S. House of Representatives, Committee on Banking and Financial Services, January 30, 1998.

Hanke, Steve H., Lars Jonung, and Kurt Schuler. *Russian Currency and Finance: A currency board approach to reform.* London, 1993.

Helander, Bernhard. "Somalia: aid fuels the conflict." Department of Cultural Anthropology Uppsala University, 1995.

Henning, Charles N. *International Financial Management.* New York: McGraw-Hill Book Co., 1978.

Hodgman, Donald R., and Geoffrey E. Wood. *Monetary and Exchange Rate Policy.* Hong Kong: Macmillan Press Ltd., 1987.

ILO. "The Role of remittances on Economy in Somalia." Report to the Mission. Nairobi, 1998.

International Crisis Group. "Somalia: Countering Terrorism in a Failed State." Nairobi, 23 May 2002.

International Financial Statistics Yearbook. *Somalia.* Washington, D.C.: IMF, 1992.

Judy, Richard W. "Currency Boards: An Idea Whose Time Has Come?" Centre for Central European and Eurasian Studies at the Hudson Institute. http://www.cipe.org/publications/fs/ert/e15/guest.htm

Krugman, Paul R., and Maurice Obstfeld. *International Economics.* Boston: Scott, Foresman and Company, 1988.

Lafrance, Robert and Simon van Norden. "Exchange rate fundamentals and the Canadian dollar." Bank of Canada Review, Spring 1995.

Latter, Tony. "The Choice of Exchange Rate Regime." *Handbooks in Central Banking* No. 2. Bank of England, London, May 1996.

Lewis, I. M. *Understanding Somalia: Guide to Culture, History, and Social Institutions.* London: Haan Associates, 1993.

Little, Peter D. "Somalia: Economy Without State." *African Issues.* Bloomington, IN: Indiana University Press, 2003.

London School of Economics and Political Science. "A Study of Decentralized Political Structures." Report commissioned by EU-EC Somali Unit. August 1995.

Mansur, Ahsan H. "Determining the Appropriate Levels of Exchange Rates for Developing Economies: Some Methods and Issues." IMF Staff Papers vol. 30 No. 4 Washington: December 1983.

McKinnon, Ronald I. and Donald J. Mathieson. "How to Manage a Depressed Economy." *Essays in International Finance* No. 145, International Finance Section, Princeton University, Princeton NJ, December 1981.

Menkhaus, Ken and John Prendergast. "Political Economy of Post-Intervention Somalia." Somalia Task Force Issue Paper # 3, April 1995.

Mohamed, Omar, Nuh Haji, and Mohamed Ali. "Exchange Rate Developments in Somalia 1970s through 1980s." Economic Research Department, Central Bank of Somalia, unpublished, 1988.

Mullei, A.K. "An analysis of the Managed Floating System for the Eternal Value of the Kenya Shilling." African Centre for Monetary Studies, Seminar on experience with instruments of economic policy in Africa, held in Addis Ababa, 30 April - 4 May 1990, unpublished.

National Post. "Company rejects Ottawa's pleas, prints money for Somali warlord." June 23, 1999.

Nichol, Peter. "The Role of the Central Bank of Bosnia and Herzegovina." Lecture to Students of the Faculty of Economics. Central Bank of Bosnia and Herzegovina, 2001.

OECD. "Exchange Rate Management and the Conduct of Monetary Policy." OECD Monetary Studies Series, Paris, 1985.

Ottawa Citizen. Interview with Prof. Mundell, July 25, 1998.

_____. "Cash printed in Canada grinds business to a halt in Somalia's capital city." September 2, 2000.

Ozumbe, C.C. (1978) *Devaluation and Balance of Payments in ECOWAS Countries: A study of Nigeria's exchange rate policy*, Central bank of Nigeria, Economic and Financial Review vol. 16 No. 1, Lagos, 1978.

Quirk, Peter J., Benedicte Vibe Christensen, Kyung-Mo Huh, and Toshiko Sasaki. "Floating Exchange Rates in Developing Countries: Experience with Auction and Interbank Markets." IMF, Occasional Papers No. 53, Washington D.C., 1987.

Roubini, Nouriel and Brad Setser. "The U.S. as Net Debtor: The Sustainability of U.S. External Imbalances." New York University. Sept. 2004.

Somaliland Times. "Borrowing From the Poor: The Cost of Uncontrolled Money Printing in Somaliland." Dr. Ismail Ibrahim Ahmed, London. June 2003.

Tabea, Zierau. *Politics and Economy in Nation-building Processes: Somaliland Republic*. University of Hanover, 2002.

Thiessen, Gordon. "The Conduct of Monetary Policy When You Live Next Door to a Large Neighbour." World Economic Affaires, Volume 3 No. 2, Autumn 2000.

Turner, Mark. "Barakat defiant after 'terror' branding by US." *Financial Times,* November 11, 2001.

United Nations Economic Commission for Africa. *Exchange Rate Management Policies in Africa: Recent Experience and Prospects.* Addis Ababa, 1995.

UNDP Somalia. Human Development Report. Nairobi, 1998.

_____. Human Development Report. Nairobi, 2001.

_____. Report on Supporting Systems and Procedures for the Effective Regulation and Monitoring of Somali Remittance Companies, 2003.

UNCTAD. "Trade And Development Report: Exchange Rate Regimes and the Scope for Regional Cooperation." New York: United Nations, 2001.

UN Security Council. *Report of the Secretary-General on the Situation in Somalia.* Various issues. 1997-2004

ABOUT THE AUTHOR

Mohamed Dalmar Abdurahman was born in Garowe, Somalia. He attended the Elementary School of Garowe and completed his intermediate and secondary education in Mogadishu.

He joined the Central Bank of Somalia in 1963. He served in many departments and branches of the Bank until he rose to the position of director general in 1989. He was a lecturer at the Somali National University, Faculty of Economics from 1981 to 1990 and taught Economic and Financial Policy to undergraduate students.

Mr. Abdurahman has B.A. (economics) from the Somali National University and MPA from the Somali National University and State University of New York at Albany. Currently, he resides in Ottawa, Canada.

www.ingramcontent.com/pod-product-compliance
Lightning Source LLC
Chambersburg PA
CBHW022024170526
45157CB00003B/1341